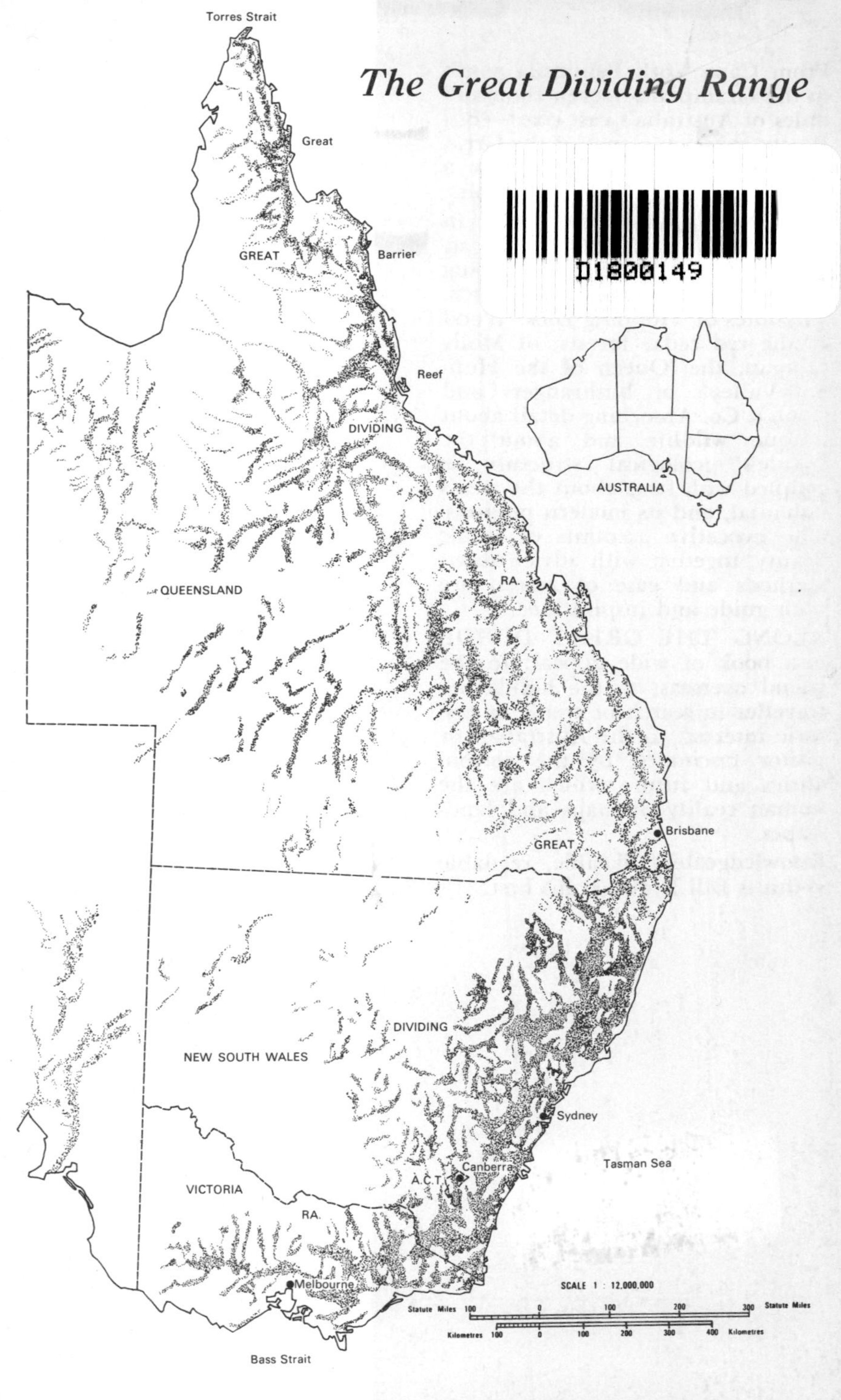
The Great Dividing Range
Torres Strait
Great
GREAT
Barrier
Reef
DIVIDING
RA.
QUEENSLAND
GREAT
Brisbane
DIVIDING
NEW SOUTH WALES
Sydney
Canberra
A.C.T.
Tasman Sea
VICTORIA
RA.
Melbourne
Bass Strait
AUSTRALIA
SCALE 1 : 12,000,000
Statute Miles 100
0
100
200
300
Statute Miles
Kilometres 100
0
100
200
300
400
Kilometres
D1800149

Along the Great Divide

Along the Great Divide

BILL BEATTY

Cassell Australia

CASSELL AUSTRALIA LTD

30-36 Curzon Street, North Melbourne, Victoria
and at

SYDNEY   LONDON   TORONTO

JOHANNESBURG   AUCKLAND

© Bill Beatty 1969
First Published 1969

SBN 304.93956.0

National Library of Australia
Registry Number Aus 68-1065

*Registered in Australia for transmission
by post as a book*

Set by Dudley E. King, Melbourne
Printed and bound by
Wilke and Company Limited, 37-49 Browns Road, Clayton, Victoria

F.769

Contents

List of Illustrations

ONE

The Cape York Country

FROM Cape York Peninsula in Australia's far north to western Victoria in the south, some 7,330 miles of highlands extend along the eastern coast of the continent as a series of mingled ranges, plateaus and high downs. Cols (or lower sections) occur between upland areas varying from 100 to 200 miles in width, their distance from the coast being anything from less than a mile in southern New South Wales to more than 100 miles in southern Queensland. This eastern highlands belt is known as the Great Dividing Range, one of the many misnomers on the Australian map which are a heritage from the original settlers and early map-makers.

It is not a range in the accepted meaning of the word; nor is it 'great' in comparison with the world's big ranges. A better title, perhaps, would be the Main Divide. No matter. These eastern highlands embrace terrain truly remarkable: mountain glory with a wealth of wild life and spectacular scenery; orchid gorges and virgin rain-forests as wild and full of wonders as a remote Brazilian jungle. And again, in contrast, enchanting bush trails, woodland waterfalls, and the undisturbed realm of Joahla the lyre-bird, Woggunba the scrub-turkey, Mibunnba the eagle. . . .

The Divide forms the chief watershed of the Commonwealth. The water divide varies considerably in character, appearing in some parts as a well-marked ridge, in others as an indefinite line on a level swampy plain, and in many parts, crossing even valley-depressions. Although it passes through the highest point in Australia, in places it is less than 1,000 feet above sea-level, and higher land may lie to the east or west of it. It is drained eastward to the coast by relatively short rivers, except in Queensland where the Burdekin and Fitzroy have carved out broad valleys and have pushed the water divide inland behind the higher coastal ranges. Westward the drainage is mainly by sluggish streams feeding into the Murray-Darling system.

Eastern Queensland is distinguished by the diversity of its landscapes. Ranges, plateaus and escarpments repeatedly alternate with valleys and lowlands. This varied belt is narrowest and most mountainous at its two extremities. Spectacular are the ranges that line the north-east coastlands between Cooktown, in the Cape York Peninsula, and Ingram. They are notched by the gorges of the Barron, Tully and Herbert rivers, and include Queensland's highest peak, Mount Bartle Frere (5,290 feet). Along the south-east border, the McPherson Range includes the striking peaks of Mount Barney and Lindesay.

Cape York Peninsula, a rough triangle of about 90,000 square miles, contains at its peak the northernmost point of the continent, Cape York. Constituting about one-eighth of Queensland's area, the region yet has half the river discharge of that State, and more than one-fourth of the total river discharge of all Australia. Such a generous volume of water makes its irrigation potential a rich one. Even at the height of the dry season water can be found anywhere about five feet below the surface; and clear pure water fills every creek and stream the year round.

While the writer was in the Peninsula recently, a group of Sydney scientists were on a five weeks' expedition covering a thousand miles of the area. Aware that fast–spreading development will destroy much of its unique wild life and natural history, the scientists brought back some 3,500 specimens of mammals, reptiles and insects, some of them hitherto unknown. Very rare specimens included wild mice which carry their young in their pouch.

The slopes of the Great Dividing Range on Cape York Peninsula are steep and precipitous, and the area is cut by narrow gorges with sides covered by screes and loose rubble. Near Cooktown are the stark Black Mountains—piles of granite covered with a thin film of iron and manganese oxides. Called Kalcajagga—and feared—by the Aboriginal tribes that once roamed the area, the mountains are honeycombed by a maze of unexplored caves and passages that have cost the lives of a number of bushmen.

One can appreciate the hardships suffered by the early pioneers when they blazed trails through this unknown land in search of gold. The opening up of the Peninsula to settlement followed the discovery of alluvial metal. In 1872, with government assistance, a systematic search for minerals was begun by William Hann, leading an expedition that traversed the headwaters of the Mitchell River and the Princess Charlotte Bay basin as far north as the Stewart River. Hann reported the existence of gold on the Palmer River; and in the following year James Venture Mulligan, a notable explorer of North Queensland, discovered rich deposits of alluvial gold on the Palmer. The rush was on. Cooktown was built in three years as the seaport for the Palmer River diggings, which uncovered fifty-five tons of gold.

> The wind is fair and free, my boys,
>   The wind is fair and free;
> The steamer's course is north, my boys,
>   And the Palmer we will see.
> And the Palmer we will see, my boys,
>   And Cooktown's muddy shore,
> Where I've been told there's lots of gold,
>   So stay down south no more.
>
> So, blow ye winds, heigho!
>   A digging we will go,
> I'll stay no more down South, my boys,
>   So let the music play.
> In spite of what I'm told,
>   I'm off in search of gold,
> And make a push for that new rush
>   A thousand miles away.

So let us make a move, my boys,
  For that new promised land,
And do the best we can, my boys,
  To lend a helping hand.
To lend a helping hand, my boys,
  Where the soil is rich and new;
In spite of blacks and unknown tracks
  We'll show what we can do.

So, with great gusto, 'The Old Palmer Song' was heard from the droves of diggers journeying from the south. Both whites and Chinese made their way to the diggings. The Chinese coolies first came to the mines in their thousands as beasts of burden, each man carrying 160 pounds on his shoulder-pole to the 120-mile distant fields. Faded photographs taken in Cooktown last century show camps of the thousands of Chinese; they were in constant fear of the Aborigines who, it was said, preferred to eat the Chinese because they were less salty than the whites.

Nearly one hundred stores and grog shanties lined the route over the wild and rugged ranges. With the advent of the railway, some of the Chinese returned to their homeland; others went into business in Cooktown opening tailoring shops, laundries, cafés and general stores. In the Cooktown State Public School is a most interesting museum of relics from the old Chinatown district. There you can see ornate screens from the josshouses, wonderfully carved in wood, with many figures of birds, animals and humans. There are incense-burners, gold- and scarlet-lacquered deities, ceremonial swords carried in front of processions to frighten the evil spirits away. The relics also include a ceremonial cooking pot, lacquered in vivid colours, which was used during feasts following the burial of friends and relatives. Food left over from the feasts was always placed on the grave for the spirit of the deceased. There is quite a collection, too, of Chinese money used during the Palmer goldrush. During this period one of Cooktown's three newspapers printed on white satin an issue listing twenty-two ships anchored in the estuary, fourteen of them from overseas. Ships from many countries called at Cooktown to load gold, tin, pearl-shell, trepang, cedar and sandalwood.

Despite the great wealth of gold officially recorded on the Palmer River fields, no one knows how much gold was won but not recorded. The Chinese smuggled gold out in the bones of dead Chinese being taken to their homeland for burial. Today the Palmer River goldfield is dead: and is part of Australia's history.

James Mulligan, the man who started it all, was an extraordinary type of explorer-prospector. He came to Australia from County Down in Ireland with his parents in 1859. He was then aged twenty, and he worked for a short while in Melbourne before trying his luck at prospecting on the Peel River goldfield in New South Wales. Later he went to New Zealand where he worked as a storekeeper, publican and gold prospector. Hearing of the gold finds in Gympie, Queensland, he returned to Australia and joined the trek to the diggings. He later went to the Etheridge goldfield near Georgetown in North Queensland.

On learning of William Hann's report of gold in the valley of the Palmer, Mulligan set out from Etheridge with a few fellow diggers to test the value of the find. They pitched camp on what was to become the site of the township of Palmerville. Three months later Mulligan's party returned to Georgetown with 102 ounces of high-grade gold; and this resulted in the great rush to the Palmer River diggings.

In 1874 Mulligan again set out in search of gold. Although he found little of it, he discovered the Hodgkinson River and the mountain which his companions named in his honour— Mount Mulligan. On a later journey Mulligan explored the Little Palmer and South Palmer rivers where he found gold deposits and started more rushes to those areas. On a fifth expedition he discovered tin on a stream which he named the Wild River. Something prompted him to return to the Hodgkinson River and investigate its area more thoroughly. As a result he uncovered gold which brought riches to the diggers and resulted in the development of Port Douglas and the city of Cairns. Mulligan also made the first discovery of silver in Queensland. This was in 1880 at a place near Herberton that became known as Silver Valley.

Mulligan had a mixed bunch of companions on some of his

expeditions, but none more strange than Christy Palmerston. Little was known of his early life, but it was claimed that he was the natural son of Lord Palmerston, Prime Minister of Great Britain, and Countess Carandini, a famous Italian opera singer and a noted beauty.

What brought Christy Palmerston to Australia is a matter of conjecture, but soon after his arrival he accompanied the James Venture Mulligan expedition to the upper Mitchell River in 1874. Despite his excellent education he was a somewhat shady character whose dealings were not always within the law, yet he was a true pioneer who did much to open up the wild, unknown country of the north.

Palmerston was a mild-mannered little man with a withered arm. He rejected civilization and chose the company of the Aborigines. No one knew where he lived and whenever he made his brief visits to the townships he wore an overcoat, cabbage-tree hat and dark glasses, and was always attended by a bodyguard of Aboriginal warriors.

His misdeeds included the robbing of the Chinese who thronged the North Queensland goldfields. They were terrified of the strange little man and his black bodyguard and always fled at his approach, leaving behind them gold which the white man promptly pocketed. A tale is told that on one occasion they laid a trap for him that nearly cost him his life. When they fled as before, Palmerston picked up one of the usual little chamois bags in which the Chinese kept their gold, and untied the draw-string. His quick eye caused him to jerk his hand away a split second before the fangs of a death-adder struck forth.

It was not only the Chinese whom Palmerston robbed. He is known to have cheated white settlers by showing them samples of gold and promising to tell them where he had found the specimens on payment of a lump sum. In this way he received considerable sums of money at various times, but there was never any gold discovered at the sites he indicated.

Christy Palmerston was responsible for subduing some of the wildest jungle natives in the Cape York Peninsula. When word reached him of the deaths of three white men speared by a tribe of these natives he set off on the trail of the killers with a rifle and his bodyguard and dealt out his own mode of justice. It was a savage form of retribution, judging by the many bullet-riddled skulls afterwards found at the site of the murders.

This remarkable little man never carried camping gear. He learned to live like the natives, and to eat whatever the bush afforded; often the roots of plants, grubs and snakes. His trail-blazing through thick jungle between the scattered white settlements opened up much territory hitherto regarded as inaccessible. He was the first white man to explore the Mulgrave, the Herbert, the Beatrice, the Tully, the North and South Johnstone, the Russell, and the Barron Rivers at their headwaters. Moreover he discovered the Daintree Pass and opened the way to Port Douglas. Today the name of this legendary 'mystery man' is remembered on the North Queensland map in the East Palmerston and West Palmerston areas and the Palmerston Highway.

On the slopes and surrounding country of the Great Dividing Range in the Cape York Peninsula there is a great wealth of plant life. This is the native haunt of many of the *Dendrobium* species of orchids including the famed Cooktown orchid. The glorious colours of the Cooktown vary in different plants, the majority being deep purple, while others range from rosy red to white. Good specimens bear flower spikes, each about eighteen inches in length, with an average of ten large long-lasting blooms.

Other beautiful and unusual orchids found in Cape York Peninsula are the *teretifolium*, or Pencil Orchid, the *speciosum*, the Ti-tree and the Bottle-brush orchids. The Pencil is a very sweetly scented variety and when in bloom the whole plant has the appearance of an exquisite wedding bouquet. The Ti-tree orchid is also sweet smelling with a honey scent that fills the air all around it. Its dainty white flowers, twenty or more to a spray, have touches of purple and yellow. The Bottle-brush orchid has unique flowers, tubular-shaped, and white in colour with pink tips and green spotted petals. The *speciosum* grows on rocks or trees of rough bark, its long sprays of waxy flowers white, cream and pale yellow, with pointed petals.

Near the Great Divide on the eastern coast of the Peninsula is the rain-forest or jungle country. In many places though the fierce tropical sun is high in a cloudless sky it fails to penetrate the canopy of treetops, the endless variety of climbing creepers and great sinuous vines as thick as a man's thigh and hanging in loops like snakes. This jungle country extends for many miles without admitting sun or the slightest breeze. The air is humid and filled with the smell of rotting trees and vegetation; yet in the semi-darkness of this sombre, sinister country picturesque life is to be found. Here are fantastically shaped and exquisitely coloured orchids; brilliantly hued birds whose magnificent plumage is accentuated by the dark surroundings; tree-climbing kangaroos; the monkey-like cuscus; cassowaries; and the largest and most powerful pythons in Australia, as long as twenty-one feet, which hang head downwards from trees near animal tracks waiting to seize their prey as it passes. The pythons are not venomous; they belong to the family of boas and are constrictors.

Tree-kangaroos are not closely related to the grazing kangaroos and wallabies but have common ancestral stock. (The only visual difference between kangaroo and wallaby is in the size. A general rule is that kangaroos have hind feet longer than 10 inches; but in fact this rule does not always apply, the feet of some kangaroos being smaller than those of large wallabies.) Most of the tree-kangaroo's life is spent in trees; for climbing, their hind feet have rough skin pads and their paws have developed strong claws.

All the kangaroo family descended from tree-dwelling stock. After adopting a terrestrial existence during which the hind-limb became elongated and the tail evolved from a prehensile organ to a balancing one, the tree-kangaroo reverted to arboreal life. As a result the limbs became more equally proportioned, the hind-feet shorter and broader, with a cushion-like roughened sole as a protection against skidding, and the nails of the fore-limbs strongly curved.

Two rather sombrely coloured species of tree-kangaroo are found here in the rain-forests of north-eastern Queensland. The teeth are adapted for the shearing and pulping of foliage and wild fruit rather than for the nipping and grinding of grasses. The animals climb or leap powerfully about among branches, and have been known to spring to the ground from heights as great as 60 feet.

The cassowary (*Casuarius*) has a number of cousins, though none outside the Australasian region. It is one of the 'big three' of this continent, the others being the emu and the jabiru. A large flightless bird, whose range is confined to these tropical jungles of North Queensland, it is shy, well camouflaged and rarely seen. Its colouration, adapted to sunless jungle, is mostly blacks and blues. Except in nesting time, it is a solitary bird, wary and secretive; it keeps to the densest parts of the jungle until evening, when it goes searching for berries, fruits and seeds. The food quest continues until daybreak.

The cassowary is characterized by a large bony helmet or casque, and by pendant red wattles on the front of its neck; otherwise the head and neck are practically naked, the skin being bright blue with an orange patch at the back of the neck. The hair-like feathers of the body (double, as are those of the emu,) bear some large hollow black spines; so too do the wing-feathers. Plumage, helmet, and the cartilaginous bone of the head act as a cushion against shock as the bird pushes its way through dense undergrowth with astonishing facility. The cassowary's powerful legs are an additional aid in forcing the body through the thickest tangle of stems and tropical climbers.

They are great jumpers and can clear at a bound an obstacle up to eight feet in height. They are pugnacious, and rival males engage in fierce battles in the jungle; but the male cassowary, like the male emu, is a devoted parent, and undertakes the task of brooding. However, since the eggs are often laid at long intervals, the female must care for one or more chicks while her partner is still on duty at the nest, incubating the remaining eggs.

The voice of the cassowary has been described as suggesting thunder in the distance; but when calling to its young its notes resemble the lowing of a cow to its calf. The loud call has been heard over a distance of three miles on a still night. The nest, which measures about three feet across, is formed of sticks and is generally built at the foot of a big tree in thick scrub. The clutch consists of three to six eggs with a granulated surface of a pea-green colour. Collectors who have been lucky enough to obtain these beautiful eggs, prize them highly.

Among the tropical birds of this region are the Gouldian finches, whose nests are illuminated by the fledglings. These magnificently hued birds build their nests in the dark fastnesses of the jungle country. The parent birds, coming from the brilliant sunshine into the dark of the forest, would have difficulty in finding and feeding their young had not nature provided the fledglings with small nodules around their mouths, giving off an opalescent colouring which glows like luminous paint.

From the rain-forest and jungle country are obtained important coniferous softwoods, including hoop pine, bunya pine and three species of kauri pine, all of which make rapid growth under plantation conditions. Other rain-forest trees yielding cabinet timbers include crow's ash, Queensland maple, cudgerie, red cedar, black bean, tulip wood, rosewood and white beech. Strangling figs are common. Beginning as seedlings on branches, these ultimately enmesh the supporting tree in a cage of roots, finally killing it, and replacing it in the form of a column of intertwined joined roots surmounted perhaps at a height of fifty feet by the branching stem proper. The stinging trees are soft-wooded giant nettles attaining, in some instances, 120 feet in height; their large leaves sting violently at the slightest touch, and the irritation may persist for weeks.

This is the country where Edmund Kennedy, the unfortunate leader of one of the most disastrous expeditions of Australian discovery, met his death together with other members of his party in 1848. Kennedy, the Assistant-Surveyor of New South Wales, in the previous year had discovered the Thompson River and established that the Barcoo River was part of Cooper's Creek. Arriving at Rockingham Bay on this tragic journey, Kennedy's party headed inland in a northerly direction and, after much privation and toil, reached Weymouth Bay where they established a depot.

Kennedy, with four others including a young Aborigine named Jackey Jackey, left this depot and made for Cape York where it had been arranged a vessel was to await them.

Terrible hardships and accidents followed, and, leaving the three men, Kennedy struggled on with the native youth. In an exhausted condition, he actually saw his goal from a peak but never reached it because a tribe of wild Aborigines closed in and speared him to death.

Jackey Jackey was wounded but escaped, and at length reached the waiting ship with Kennedy's precious journal. Rescue parties set out for the depot at Weymouth Bay where six of the eight left there were found dead through starvation; the other three men were never seen again. Jackey Jackey, a man named Goddard, and the 25-year old botanist, Carron, who was later appointed to the staff of the Sydney Botanic Gardens, were the sole survivors. The young Aborigine is commemorated in the naming of a stream near the tip of Cape York Peninsula, and an airstrip known as Jackey Jackey was built on the peninsula during World War II; it was the most northerly airfield in Australia.

TWO

The Atherton Tableland

To the south of the Cape York country lies a plateau of the Great Dividing Range known as the Atherton Tableland. Rising sharply from a narrow coastal plain, this scarp is very rugged and steep with many deep gorges and sharp ridges which rise in places to more than 5,000 feet. It represents one of the few areas of true mountain landscape in the highlands. Here the peak called Mount Bartle Frere—the highest point in the State—rears above the Bellenden-Ker Range. Bartle Frere was named after a president of the Royal Geographical Society. Its vegetation, like that of its companion peaks, is largely tropical rain-forest; and it carries a considerable variety of distinctive plants, birds and mammals.

The boundaries of the Atherton Tableland are indefinite but its area, situated generally between the Palmer River and the headwaters of the Burdekin, is usually estimated at 12,000 square miles and its average height at 2,500 feet.

From the south the Atherton Tableland is reached via the Palmerston Highway where you drive through rain-forests of giant trees, some acting as 'hosts' to staghorn ferns and orchids. Tremendous vines of many types trail from the branches. If you stop occasionally you will be rewarded with the call and song of the hundreds of birds which are found in these dense forests. All flora and fauna are protected. In a sudden and unexpected change of scenery you see before you rolling green hills and valleys, grazing cattle, fields of maize sometimes ten feet in height, tobacco farms with their neat homes, or the famous Tolga peanuts. All this can be viewed from the main road.

For the traveller to the Tablelands from Cairns there are two routes, one of which takes you up the Gillies Highway. It winds up 2,700 feet giving superb views of the sugar lands below, until you find yourself practically at the entrance of Lake Barrine, one of the crater lakes. The alternative is the delightful trip on the Lilliputian narrow-gauge rail motor from Cairns to Kuranda and then by road. From the depths of Barron Gorge, the little train snakes its way up through verdant forest aisles, through dark tunnels, and over crashing, foaming cascades to quaint Kuranda, whose floral railway station is the prettiest in Australia. Countless ferns and staghorns, orchids and tropical plants adorn the full length of the station, and one could cheerfully miss the train, lost in admiration of such loveliness. In North Queensland alone there are 170 species of orchid known to be native to the area.

Kuranda is on the threshold of the Atherton Tableland; and whether you are travelling by rail or road, the Kuranda district is well worth a prolonged halt. From the railway—a masterpiece of engineering skill, skirting the very edge of the Barron Gorge—unfold magnificent views of neatly patterned cane fields with roads and streams criss-crossing in intricate design, and of dense tropical scrub interlaced with cascading waters. The Barron Falls are a fraction under two miles over a good road from Kuranda, and a parking area overlooks the river's plunge into the turbulent depths hundreds of feet below.

Most Tableland tours visit the prosperous towns of Atherton, Mareeba, Malanda, and the lovely lakes of Barrine and Eacham. Mareeba is the Tobacco Capital of Australia, its sales of tobacco in a year reaching some sixteen million dollars. From the road, tobacco fields can be seen with the curing barns in close proximity, and busy hands picking the tobacco leaf during the season. Many languages will be heard as you walk down Mareeba's main street; this is a progressive town of nearly 6,000 people from various parts of the world, particularly Italy. A number of industries are found in this area, and there are large cattle yards on the outskirts where thousands of beasts pass through from all over the Gulf country.

The town of Atherton derives its name from John Atherton, early pioneer and settler in the district. In 1880, with the finding of tin in this area, the first influx of people into the district began. Settlements sprang up at scattered points; but their growth was chequered and uncertain, waxing and waning with the fortunes of the fields. Stability and security were ensured with the tillage of the soil—the growing of maize. Later the unparalleled success of this venture centralized the settlement of the town in its present location. The Atherton area is acknowledged the richest maize-growing one in the Commonwealth, the average yield approximately thirty-two bushels per acre. Peanut-growing is also one of the district's major industries and a source of great wealth to Atherton.

The town is in the centre of the Tableland proper and is recognized as the 'capital' of that area, with the port of Cairns as base. Its climate is superb, with a mild summer and bright and sunny winter days; throughout the year the nights are delightfully cool and bracing. Atherton was developed under a town-planning scheme, and is served by good water and electricity supplies. Spacious recreation grounds embrace bowling greens, golf course and an Olympic swimming pool. The modern and substantial business premises of this progressive town are a pointer to the faith of the business community in the prosperity of the district.

Lake Barrine is a placid, serene sheet of water lined with blue water-lilies against a background of dense jungle growth, giant kauri pines, maples, cedars and wild fig trees. During a stay at Lake Barrine I observed an old Aborigine raking up leaves in a garden. His employer told me that this native was the last of a cannibal tribe who killed their enemies for the sole purpose of obtaining their kidneys, the eating of which, they believed, gave them greater strength and power. When this particular native was caught in the act by the police troopers he was given a life imprisonment, but after some years was freed. Becoming attached to his former gaoler, he never returned to the bush but settled down in the ways of civilization.

From Lake Barrine to Lake Eacham, a few miles farther on, the road traverses some of the most beautiful forest country on the Tableland. A notice requests motorists to reduce speed as bush turkeys, pheasants, and many other birds and animals may be seen crossing the road, which passes through a tropical jungle. The crater lake itself is surrounded by thick vegetation and a walk along a well-defined path round the waters enables one to appreciate much of its beauty. Turtles can be seen in one particular area, and seem to enjoy the company of visitors, particularly if they bring a slice or two of bread with them.

The Tinaroo Falls Dam on the Barron River is eleven miles north-east from Atherton, and twenty-three air miles across the mountains from Cairns. Water from the dam is gravitated through 200 miles of main channel and through a similar mileage of distribution channels in areas where lack of water had caused setbacks and failures in the pioneering days of tobacco growing. One of Queensland's most important developments, the Tinaroo Falls Dam, impounds the waters of the Barron River to form a lake two-thirds the size of Sydney Harbour, and holding three-quarters as much water. It irrigates 38,000 acres of land on the Atherton Tableland and has sufficient water to maintain regular irrigation supplies through six years of drought. Tinaroo, incidentally, is not an Aboriginal word. According to records of the district Jack Atherton, after whom Atherton is named, was prospecting with another miner when they made a happy discovery. Atherton threw his hat in the air and shouted 'Tin Hurroo!'

Inland the Atherton Plateau resembles the Blue Mountains of New South Wales in having a flat skyline, and being severely dissected into canyon-like gorges. Here is found the Musk-rat kangaroo, the smallest of all the hopping marsupials in Australia. Its head and body measures only about 12 inches in length and its tail about 6 inches. Little is known about this tiny hopper's habits. It is, however, believed to be mostly diurnal which is not common among the smaller macropods. (The Macropodidae, the largest ground-dwelling, grass-feeding marsupial family in the world, includes all the kangaroo-like animals of Australia, the pademelon wallabies, rock wallabies, hare-wallabies, rat-kangaroos, potoroos, tree-kangaroos, brush wallabies and many others.)

The Musk-rat kangaroo has a naked scaly tail and differs from all other living macropods in that it has five fingers and five toes. All other kangaroo-like animals have four toes. The only member of its sub-family, it is regarded as a primitive link with the family of phalangers (pouched animals such as possums, which live up trees, and feed on honey, flowers or foliage). It has dental similarities, together with its sub-equal limbs, its tail, and its being the only species in the family with a movable first or great toe. It feeds almost entirely on insects and their larvae, and its musky odour is probably caused by its diet.

Much has been written about the larger kangaroos. It seems a pity, however, that little or no publicity has been given to many of the smaller species, such as the Musk-rat kangaroo— which is confined solely to the Atherton Tableland region and the rain-forests of north-eastern Queensland.

Tucked away in the tin-bearing country of the rugged ranges are towns that are towns in name only. Now far off the beaten track, these rich and populous centres of less than a century ago are unvisited by strangers who are unaware of their existence. These forgotten boom towns include Stannary Hills, Watsonville, Ravenswood and Irvinebank. The latter is about twenty miles from Herberton, a sleepy-hollow community that seems to be living in the past. To get there one has to travel an extremely rough road, and there are two steep ranges to negotiate.

The main street of Irvinebank is lined with deserted two-storeyed buildings of brick and decaying wood, with shutters falling off their rusted hinges. A conspicuous structure is the School of Arts Hall whose interior reveals a large dance-floor and a fine stage; a pathetic sight being the tattered drop-curtains and the torn, faded scenery. Handbills on the musty walls advertise the visit of theatrical companies of bygone days. It is even more depressing to see the once well-stocked library of more than two thousand books all mouldering into dust; they crumble at the mere touch. Outside the School of Arts Hall there used to be a large lawn where musical programmes were regularly given by the town's two brass bands, the winners of many a North Queensland band contest and music festival.

A shallow and silted dam formed by a wall of logs across a creek is a relic of a site which in the early 1900s was deep and wide enough for boat-races to be held there. Below the dam is the former sportsground, the scene of football and cricket fixtures hotly contested by teams drawn from all over the far north.

Tin was discovered at Irvinebank in 1880. One of the first mines there was opened by John Moffat, a young Scotsman; and the town was named in honour of his birthplace. Tin-mining became a major industry in Queensland, and Irvinebank developed into one of the State's most important towns, owing to this Scottish migrant's enterprise. His company built a twenty-five mile private railway linking Irvinebank with the main line between Cairns and Chillagoe; and it carried, besides passengers and merchandise, tens of thousands of pounds' worth of tin ingots. Mines other than that of John Moffat produced vast quantities of tin for many years; more than a million dollars' worth was brought forth for example, by the Vulcan (1,500 feet), the deepest mine in Australia.

With John Moffat's ultimate retirement, and the outbreak of World War I, the Queensland Government took over the smelters; but by this time the price of tin was dropping considerably and production fell off to a degree that hastened the departure of large numbers of people from the district. The population continued to dwindle, mines were closed, and eventually the rail line was pulled up.

The high altitude of Irvinebank gives it a bracing climate. The air is crisp and clear, even in summertime, and its surrounding panorama of dramatic peaks and valleys is most impressive. Despite the forlorn fate of the township, one easily appreciates the optimistic outlook of those convinced that with modern machinery and government encouragement, these ancient hills may yet yield more than all their past wealth.

The township of Ravenswood rusts quietly, with cattle and billy goats wandering its main streets. Its permanent population of twenty have 30-room hotels, churches, shops, halls, and a police and an ambulance station, all to themselves. Tall chimneys, mullock heaps and winding gear encircle the town, but silence hangs over all. The big bible on the lectern of the Methodist Church—with its faded Gothic inscription 'The just shall live by faith'—is white-anted; and the empty tabernacle of the Catholic Church is another mute reminder of vanished congregations.

In the days of its former glories the gold-mining town had 40,000 inhabitants and forty-two licensed pubs to cool their throats and warm their dreams. Ravenswood is reached from Townsville by travelling fifty-six miles along the Burdekin Highway to Mingela and another twenty-seven miles south to the town. It was a sad day, the proprietress of the Imperial Hotel will inform you, when they took their train away. They pulled up the track, every inch of it, every sleeper. But, she assures you, Ravenswood will come good again: the Broken Hill Proprietary has taken up leases on forty-two square miles around the town. They must have something in mind. Gold? Molybdenum?

In the meantime, Ravenswood really comes to life once a year at Hallow-e'en, when hundreds of former residents and visitors make the trek from Townsville and elsewhere to attend a big party, dressed, appropriately, as ghosts and wraith-like figures.

Here in the North miners are still fossicking for tin, copper, gold, silver and many other minerals. One hears of big finds of sapphires, opals and the like. For many years, agates have been collected by people living in the area from which they come; they have either sent them south or sold them locally. Agates of North Queensland are second to none in the world, their beauty and remarkable colouring reminding one of an artist's palette.

Near Forsayth is an area known as Agate Creek, but originally called Sinbad's Valley. For the visitor a four-wheel drive vehicle is to be recommended; and either a guide or a map of the area is a 'must'. The road most of the way is unsealed and, after Forsayth, there is a bare track which may or may not be discernible. All supplies, including water, are an essential part of your gear.

The ideal period to plan a visit is just after the 'wet', when the rain will have uncovered these brilliant agate rocks. There are many other places for fossicking, such as the Chillagoe and Mount Surprise areas; but wherever you go, go prepared. Gem stones of all descriptions can be found, some of which are sapphires, garnets and topaz. This part of Australia is the lapidary's paradise.

Mount Garnet was so named because of the great quantity of garnets found in the area. On the Mount Garnet road, twenty-five miles from Ravenshoe, stands the Innot Hot Springs Hotel with its own mining museum. Local minerals are included, together with specimens from all over the world. Oddest of the exhibits in this valuable collection is a set of false teeth: tin teeth made by an old tin-miner living in the district.

Before he made them he used to wear the orthodox type of dentures, but found them uncomfortable and decided to do his own dentistry, although he had no dental training. The tin teeth were a great success, and he wore them for years; even professional dentists have pronounced them splendidly made and finished. The old fellow made a fair amount of money out of his tin-mining, but he always spent it at the hotel. When he hadn't any more left, out would come his teeth to be handed to the barman as security for a few more drinks. When meal time came, he would borrow his teeth back, but would always return them until the next meal hour, or until he had paid off his debt. In his will he bequeathed them to the hotel's museum.

The little town of Chillagoe, at an altitude of 1,156 feet, is the centre of an old mining field that has produced great quantities of copper, tin, silver-lead and other minerals. Now the smelters are closed in this former '10 pub town', the population has dwindled to a few fossickers and 'rock hounds', and the district is little more than a centre for the surrounding cattle stations. Chillagoe is remarkable for its extensive limestone deposits which, on weathering, give rise to an extraordinary topography—life-like formations of large animals, including an elephant, and massive figures reminiscent of Henry Moore sculptures. There are totally unexplored limestone masses, many square miles in extent; and it is certain that many caves, much larger than those already known, remain to be discovered. Some of the big caves and chains of caves with stalactite and stalagmite formations equal to any in Australia, have been made accessible. One chamber in the Royal Arch Cave has a length of 170 feet, a breadth of more than 100 feet, and a height of 40 feet.

THREE

Golden Towns

From the Atherton Plateau to the New South Wales border the highlands consist of rolling downlands with broad, mature valleys and occasional residual mountain peaks and flat-topped ridges. On the coastal side these uplands are fringed by wild, fractured country of the Cape York type.

On an eastern arm of the Great Dividing Range, some eighty miles south-west of Townsville and more than a thousand feet above sea-level lies Charters Towers. 'The Towers', as it is better known in the North, is the centre of what was for many years the most famous goldfield in Queensland, which produced wealth to the value of over $60 million. The name appears in several ballads that evolved on the diggings:

> 'You were not the cleanest potato, Dan Holt,
>   And you hadn't the cleanest of fins,
> But you made your pile on 'The Towers', Dan Holt,
>   And that covers most of your sins.'

The word Charters was the name of one of the district's pioneers, Warden W. S. Charters. Originally Charters Tors ('tors' is a Cornish word meaning hills), the name was later changed to Charters Towers. The 7,000 people of the district are only one-fifth of the population that was Charters Towers' at the turn of the century, and at that time there were no more than half a million people in the whole of Queensland.

This 'Golden Age' lasted for more than a quarter of a century, when Charters Towers boasted of its four newspapers, fifty-eight hotels, and several theatres visited by theatrical companies from Sydney and Melbourne. The cab-stand at the railway station was its pride and joy: fifty or sixty horse cabs, all of them four-wheelers, awaited the arrival of every train as though they expected vice-regal visitors. Every cab, spic and span with its metal fittings gleaming, was drawn by perfectly groomed horses always in pairs and matched like twins. Distinguished visitors were invariably given four-in-hand blacks, and whites were kept for wedding parties.

Those were the swaggering days when the residents referred to Charter Towers not as a mere town or city but as 'The World'! The World has diminished a good deal since 1916, when the last big mine in the district closed. One of the streets —Craven Street—is named after a plucky prospector of that name who stuck to it when everything seemed black, in the days before the district gained its wealth pledging his future on a come-back for his claims. He was lucky, and his persistence gave the town a fresh fillip.

With the decline of mining, Charters Towers has become the main centre of a considerable pastoral, dairying, and citrus-growing district, and is noted for its educational establishments. Some 1,400 students, most of them boarders from far-flung places, attend six State and church colleges with park-like grounds and extensive playing fields. The climate is considered to be the healthiest in all Queensland. A seismograph station established by the Queensland University on Towers Hill is one of the most modern in the world, and has further enhanced Charters Towers' prestige as a seat of education and science.

On the Great Dividing Range, 228 miles from Rockhampton, is Clermont, another town with a golden past: but with many gold claims still being worked in the area. Today the town is the centre of a rich mineral, pastoral and agricultural district. Twelve miles away at Blair Athol extensive coal deposits occur. One of them, estimated at more than 200 million tons, is the largest known deposit of black coal in the southern hemisphere. The seam ranges from 15 to 93 feet in thickness, with a shallow overburden, and extends for approximately five square miles.

Clermont is also the centre of a large area of State forests, and considerable quantities of hardwood for building materials and railway sleepers are cut in its sawmills. One of the features of the district is Peak Range, which is composed of a number of isolated heights of which Wolfang Peak is the most striking. An immense natural obelisk, 1,000 feet high, the peak rises out of a mountain standing alone near the centre of a large expanse of undulating downs.

A century has passed since Clermont gained wide notoriety when the former gold commissioner of the district murdered two troopers for the sake of the £8,000 they were assisting him to take to safety.

A number of Clermont people had petitioned the Government in Sydney requesting the transfer of Gold-Commissioner John Thomas Griffin. In this they were successful and he was removed to Rockhampton. Griffin, a former police magistrate, was a heavy gambler who lived far above his means and who, in preference to paying his debts, usually called out his creditors to a bout of boxing or broadswords, in both of which he was highly skilled.

Within a short while of his arrival in Rockhampton a group of Chinese approached him and demanded money for a parcel of gold which they had entrusted to him a few months earlier in Clermont. They threatened him with exposure for mis-appropriating the gold unless the money was forthcoming. To their joyful surprise Griffin was able to pay them in full settlement.

Three days earlier, in his capacity of Assistant-Goldfields Commissioner, Griffin sent his subordinate, Sergeant Julian, to collect over £8,000 from the manager of the Australian Stock Bank for conveyance to Clermont. Using the presence of bushrangers on the route as an excuse, Griffin took the unusual step of personally accompanying the escort of two troopers. During the journey a shot from Griffin's pistol tore through trooper Power's tunic, grazing his body. The Assistant-Commissioner said it was an accident. In a chance encounter the following day, Power mentioned this 'accident' to another policeman. He also told how he and the other trooper had brewed a billy of tea and found it bitter-tasting. They had thought the bitterness due to green twigs falling into the billy;

but when they threw the contents away, they discovered a whitish powder in the bottom of the billy.

Later, when the bullet-ridden bodies of the two troopers were found near the Mackenzie River, Griffin said that bushrangers must have shot them and stolen the money while he was absent from the scene. After a police investigation, the Assistant-Goldfields Commissioner was arrested and brought to trial. His conviction resulted from evidence including the story of the bitter-tasting tea, and that told by the Chinese, recalled from Sydney just as they were embarking for China. It was proved that they were paid with notes from one of the bags entrusted to Griffin by the bank before the escort's departure. Judge Lutwyche, remarking that he had never heard a case so clearly proved by weight of circumstantial evidence, sentenced Griffin to death.

The former Goldfields Commissioner, after murdering the two troopers, had secreted the rest of the bank's money in a marked spot near Rockhampton. Before his execution, he tried to use his knowledge of its hiding-place to bribe two warders to allow him to escape. The money, eventually, was found after his death. Incidentally, Griffin's skull was stolen from his grave and exhibited by a Rockhampton doctor for many years.

A branch railway line takes you from Clermont to the town of Emerald, through which passes the Tropic of Capricorn. The raising of sheep and cattle is the mainstay of the district, but it also grows a variety of agricultural products including cotton, sorghum, wheat, maize, citrus and other fruits.

The Commonwealth Government recently announced that it was making available up to $20 million for the Emerald Dam scheme. This is a non-repayable grant for a major dam to be built on the Nogoa River at Emerald; the Queensland Government will be expected to finance the scheme's irrigation and associated works. The project is designed to irrigate about 45,000 acres for crops and also to provide relief for stock from other areas of the State during drought. The Queensland Government has submitted the Emerald project as its first priority, under the northern development programme.

Following the Great Divide south, the next place of

importance is Springsure, at an altitude of 1,100 feet. The district has an impressive landscape with rugged peaks and bluffs of volcanic origin. The town derives its name from the fact that it grew at the foot of a bold mass of rocks from which springs ran down. On a visit to Springsure, Lady Brassey, the wife of a Queensland Governor, saw in the rough the opals which she afterwards purchased in London for two hundred guineas. Cattle-raising is the principal industry, and there is good agricultural land in the area.

On Cullin-la-ringo, a pastoral property at Springsure, took place the bloodiest massacre of white settlers by Aborigines in Australia's history. In 1861 Horatio Wills and a party of men, women and children—22 in all—arrived on the property after a ten months' trek from Victoria. They seemed to have cultivated good relations with the neighbouring tribes, and had been there only two weeks when the massacre occurred.

On the day of the attack three of the new settlers were on a distant part of the property, and these were the only ones to escape. The victims were taken by surprise. Wills's body was found in a tent; the shepherds, clubbed and speared to death, lay near their sheep; and one of the slain bullock-drivers still held his whip in his hand. The murdered women were found in the attitude of sewing; the cook's body was near the fire-place. This was the scene that met the eyes of the shocked men when they returned to the plundered huts and tents.

Deserters from the native police force's trackers were named as the ringleaders of the massacre; and a punitive force set out immediately. A terrible reprisal followed, and tribes of Aborigines were almost exterminated in this and other areas.

West of Springsure is a spur of the Great Divide known as the Warrego Range. These mountains extend in a mainly south-westerly direction for about 100 miles, to near the town of Blackall. The range forms the division between the upper waters of the Warrego River to the south and the Barcoo River to the north. 'On the Upper Barcoo where churches are few, and men of religion are scanty . . .' or, as another ballad has it, 'On the far Barcoo, where they eat nardoo, a thousand miles away . . .' (Reduced to a flour-like substance, the native plant, nardoo, is used for food by Aborigines.)

The McPherson Range, a spur of the Great Divide, Queensland–
New South Wales   (page 35)

Relics from the old Chinatown district at the Cooktown State School museum   (page 4)

The Warrego Range and the river of the same name were first explored by Sir Thomas Mitchell in 1846, when he set forth on an expedition to tropical Australia from Parramatta in New South Wales. At the outset of the great trek he had 76 men, 8 drays, 80 bullocks, 2 boats, 17 horses, 3 carts, 250 sheep, and provisions for a year.

Mitchell had served with great distinction in the Peninsular war; hence the names on the Australian map identified with this campaign. It must be admitted, however, that he once gave orders, as Surveyor-General, that no river, creek, mountain, valley or plain should be named other than by its native name without his express permission. Mitchell was a scholar, writer and inventor, patenting a steamer propeller. His son, Roderick, aged 27, was to have had charge of an expedition searching for the lost explorer Leichhardt; travelling by sea from Newcastle to Sydney, however, he fell overboard and was drowned.

Ten miles south of the Tropic of Capricorn and east of the Great Dividing Range is the outstanding mining area of Mount Morgan. Located in the Dee Range, the town and mountain is Queensland's principal producer of gold, and an important source of copper. The town of Mount Morgan, which exists solely on account of the mine, is built on the slopes of a valley adjacent to the ore-bearing mountain. When discovered, this was a rocky mount set amongst a tangle of peaks and ridges, and was named 'Ironstone Mountain' owing to the nature of its surface. After many years of intensive working it resembles a great volcanic crater.

The area was originally selected by John Gordon in 1870 as a grazing property, the western boundary fence of which crossed the top of the Mount. Eight years later Donald Gordon, son of the original selector, acquired the freehold title to the property. Soon afterwards Donald's brother, Alexander, introduced the Morgan brothers, Thomas and Edwin, for whom he was working on the Cawarral goldfield. Failing to discover a mineral 'show' to which they were being led by Alexander, they took refuge in a hut on the Gordon property during torrential rain. When the deluge abated they were unable to return by the usual route because the creeks were running bankers; and, as they passed some black boulders outside the property, Edwin knocked a few pieces off them. On examination, he said that he thought they contained more gold than stone.

One of the Morgans sent a sample to Gympie for assay and the report gave 3,700 ounces to the ton. The Morgans were joined by another brother, Frederick, and together they pegged out as much as they were able outside Gordon's property, meantime re-naming the site 'Mount Morgan'. In 1884 they sold out their interests for a fortune, and a limited liability company was established. Thereafter the production of gold rose sharply. During this period a number of un-successful attempts were made to 'jump' the claim and led to a series of unsuccessful lawsuits. Out of the Mount Morgan mine has come millions in dividends, a goodly portion of which have been used in the extension of industry and to assist in the advancement of Australian culture.

The Maranoa River rises on the Buckland Tableland, on the south-western side of the Great Dividing Range, and runs southward for about 330 miles before joining the Balonne River. The name Maranoa was given by Sir Thomas Mitchell, and is said to be an Aboriginal word meaning a hand, which was applied to a section of the river and its creeks that resembled the shape of a human hand. The name Maranoa has also been given to an extensive pastoral and agricultural district, of which Roma is one of the principal towns.

Roma, on the Great Divide, honours the name of the Countess Diamantina Bowen, daughter of Count Roma, a noble of an ancient Venetian family. She became the wife of George Ferguson Bowen, the first Governor of Queensland and a scholar of note. The Countess is also honoured in the naming of Queensland's Mount Diamantina and the Diamantina River.

Wheat, grapes and citrus fruit are grown around Roma, and its industries include a butter-factory, flour-mill, and winery. More than a century has passed since Queensland's first vineyard was established at Roma and where was produced the first wine to be sold in the State. The town is a cattle-selling centre and the Roma area itself is a potential oil-bearing one.

Until recent times the history of the search for petroleum or oil in Australia has been mostly a tale of hard work, high expenditure, and disappointment. Petroleum is composed almost entirely of carbon and hydrogen, the atoms of which are joined together in an endless variety of molecules to form hydrocarbons. It occurs naturally as a gas (natural gas), as liquids of varying viscosity (crude oil), and as a solid (bitumen, tar, or pitch). The Australian colonies had been importing petroleum products from North America for thirty years before men began to look for oil in Australia. In 1892, the first bore was sunk in the Coorong area of South Australia where masses of 'coorongite' (then thought to indicate the presence of oil) had been discovered forty years earlier. No trace of oil was found.

Here at Roma natural gas was accidentally discovered in 1900 when an artesian water bore was being deepened. Further holes were sunk in the area, but no oil was found. The gas from the first Roma well went to waste until 1906 when a reticulation system was completed. Natural gas lit the streets of Roma for ten days before the flow failed. Two years later a new bore struck gas at 3,700 feet. The gas caught fire and flared spectacularly for six weeks until a giant 'candle-extinguisher' was used to put out the blaze.

In 1954 drilling in the Roma district struck natural gas at the rate of 1.5 million cubic feet a day. It was not until six years later, however, that new reserves of gas were found in the district. In 1963 a new gas field, with a proven initial recoverable reserve of 39,000 million cubic feet, was found at Bony Creek, 15 miles south-east of Roma. In the same year another strike was announced at Richmond, about nine miles from Roma—an oil/gas field with a proven initial recoverable reserve of 87,000 barrels of oil, 14,000 million cubic feet of gas. And in early 1964 came the announcement of yet another major gas flow north of Roma.

It was from the Roma district, in April 1848, that the Prussian explorer Ludwig Leichhardt set out on his last journey, which remains one of the chief mysteries of the

Australian bush. The 34-year old leader and his party intended to travel north for some distance before striking due west, and then heading south along the coast of Western Australia to Perth. Unfortunately, Leichhardt's companions were neither competent nor experienced. His associates were limited to a relative named Adolf Classen, a stockman named Arthur Hentig, two hired men—Stewart and Kelly, and two 'tame' Aborigines.

When the party left a station property near the site of the present town of Roma it was calculated that the journey would occupy about two years, but in fact neither provisions nor horses were sufficient for such a lengthy period. From that time the fate of the party—and of its 77 animals—has remained unknown. Despite the number of other expeditions sent out to search for the lost party, not one definite relic has ever been recovered.

On the western slopes of the Great Divide is Dalby, 153 miles by rail from Brisbane and 1,126 feet above sea-level. Named after a town on the Isle of Man, Dalby is a well-planned town with attractive public and private buildings. It is the centre of a large pastoral, agricultural and dairying district, and is a popular health resort. This is part of the rich Darling Downs country, of which Toowoomba is the 'capital'. Much of the scenery of the region, comprising an area of about 5,625 square miles of fertile black-soil plains and valleys, is very beautiful. Its rolling downs of grain fields and lush grazing pastures, with their flocks of sheep and prize herds of cattle, delight the eye. Here grows some of the finest wheat in all Australia, and yields of 69 bushels an acre have been recorded. The farms are almost entirely mechanized, for both planting and harvesting; and the grain is mostly handled in bulk.

The Darling Downs were discovered in 1827 by Allan Cunningham, the botanist (Dalby's main thoroughfare, Cunningham Street, was named in his honour). Notwithstanding his glowing accounts of the district, settlement did not begin until thirteen years later. In the pioneering days there were many clashes with the Aborigines. Most of these early conflicts were matters of reprisal, on one side or the other, between those defending their sacred grounds or their women-folk, and the newcomers objecting to their stock being speared or stolen. The attitude in most cases was that if a black killed a white it was murder, but when whites killed blacks it was 'teaching them a lesson'.

In 1873 a report of a bunyip being seen in the district came from Dalby. It was described as 'having a head like a seal, and a tail consisting of two fins, a larger and a smaller one'. Despite some local variations, the story of the bunyip has so much in common throughout a considerable part of Australia that it is fair to assume that the myth had a basis in some common act of Natural History.

The bunyip of the Queensland Aborigines was a large, dark-coloured, furred animal, with glowing eyes and a bellowing call, a haunter of swamps and billabongs. The imagination of the Victorian natives around Port Phillip pictured the bunyip as a fearsome booming beast, as big as a bullock, with an emu's neck, the mane and tail of a horse, and a seal's flippers. It had a cuckoo's instinct, and laid turtle's eggs in the nest of a platypus. Strangely enough, the description fits very closely that extinct marine reptile the plesiosaurus. The natives believed that the bunyip would engulf solitary fishermen, canoe and all, in its mighty jaws and then sink like a stone to its undiscoverable den. An early Australian writer mentioned that six Aborigines preferred death by bushfire to taking shelter in a waterhole believed to be the home of a bunyip.

It did not take the white man long to get interested in the bunyip. The first official reference, indicating a pre-knowledge, appeared in the minutes of the Geographical Society of Australia, on 19 December, 1821. Following the report by the explorer Hamilton Hume of the existence of a strange animal in Lake Bathurst, supposedly a manatee, hippopotamus, or bunyip, the suggestion was recorded that Hume be reimbursed for expenditure incurred in any further attempt to obtain hide, teeth or other tangible evidence of the existence of this creature.

In the early days of Victoria, before it became a separate colony, Governor La Trobe wrote that there were 'two kinds' of bunyip. He sent drawings of the 'southern' kind to Tasmania, but they may have been lost. The following news item appeared in the Melbourne *Morning Herald* of 29 October, 1849:

'The Veritable Bunyip has been seen at last! We are informed by Mr Edwards, the managing clerk at the office of Messrs Moor and Chambers, that during his late trip, and making the circuit of Phillip Island, he and his party were astonished at observing an animal sitting upon a bank in a lake.

'The animal is described as being from six to seven feet long and, in general appearance, half man and half baboon.

'Five shots were fired, and the last discharge was replied to by a spring into the air, and a contemptuous fling out of the hind legs, and a final disappearance in the placid waters of the lake. A somewhat long neck, feathered like an emu, was the peculiar characteristic of the animal.'

Thirty miles north-east of Dalby is the Bunya Mountains National Park of more than 24,000 acres, from which there are considerable views over the Darling Downs and the eastern plateau. The magnificent bunya pine forest, from which the region gets its name, is preserved in all its primeval splendour. These mountains were once the territory of the Waka Waka tribe, but other tribes came here regularly from hundreds of miles around to feast on the milky white bunya nuts. There are still relics of these lengthy feasts, during which all laws on tribal boundaries were suspended and there was peace between the tribes.

The large sweetish seeds were an important article of food to the Aborigines, who roasted them; every third year the seed crop was very plentiful and it was then that the natives assembled for the feasts. Today this tall coniferous tree is frequently planted for ornament, because of its immense dome-shaped crown and symmetrical sweeping branches. It also yields a valuable timber very easily worked and eminently suitable for joinery, cabinet-work and plywood.

Apart from the bunya pine forest in this National Park, there is open hardwood forest of red gum and yellow stringy-bark, rain-forest with conifers, and the stunted species of backhousia scrub merging at lower levels with bottle trees and native cypress. Ancient grass-trees are a feature of the Bunya Mountains whose miles of graded tracks lead from access points to hidden waterfalls, lookouts and shady groves.

FOUR

The Darling Downs

On the rim of the Great Dividing Range at an altitude of some 2,000 feet, and less than 100 miles from Brisbane, stands Queensland's largest inland city and the chief commercial centre of the Darling Downs. Toowoomba is a clean, uncluttered city with an atmosphere of prosperous contentment. It calls itself 'The Garden City' and its many fine parks and gardens, together with tree-shaded streets, justify the title. The city's annual Carnival of Flowers is held in September and attracts an influx of visitors to swell a population of around 54,000.

Although Toowoomba's initial development came entirely from primary industries, it now has a solid core of secondary industries, resulting in a sound and balanced economy. The Toowoomba Foundry, established in 1871, is claimed to be the largest foundry in the southern hemisphere. Notable men born and educated in Toowoomba include the statesman Sir Littleton E. Groom, the journalist and literary critic A. G. Stephens, and artist J. J. Hilder. Two other men of letters were born in the district: Arthur H. Davis ('Steele Rudd') and George Essex Evans.

Scenic features of Toowoomba include Picnic Point, a bluff spur of the Main Range on whose summit the city stands; and Table Top Mountain, lying near the foot of the Toll Bar. In its early years the settlement at Toowoomba was known as 'The Swamp'. Archdeacon Benjamin Glennie preached at The Swamp in 1848, using the largest room in a local inn for his sparsely attended services. He apparently disliked the name of the settlement, and at nearby Drayton in 1852 he baptized children whose parents were entered in the register as residing at Toowoomba, the Aboriginal name for the district. The name received the endorsement of settlers at a sports gathering on New Year's Day, 1858, when it was displayed in white letters on a sheet of red calico and erected at the winning post. Incidentally, Drayton was originally called Dray Town from the large number of drays seen there in pioneering days. 'Steele Rudd', author of *On Our Selection*, assisted his father there in his blacksmithing business.

South of Toowoomba, in the Darling Downs district, lie Cunningham's Gap, Warwick and Killarney. Cunningham's Gap, named in honour of the explorer, was discovered in 1828 when Cunningham was seeking a route from the coast to the Darling Downs across the Great Dividing Range. The Gap itself is a deep saddle between two peaks, each about 4,000 feet, in an area of dense rain-forest passing into mixed and open forest at higher levels.

More than 14 miles of graded walking tracks lead to the mountain crests which overlook the rugged slopes of that part of the Great Divide and the farmlands of the Fassifern Plain. Along these hiking tracks are giant spear lilies, wild orchids, avenues of plumed grass-trees, hanging gardens of rock lilies, staghorns, elkhorns and dense groves of piccabeen palms. Of strange appearances are the grass-trees—in Western Australia they are called blackboys. They have a thick stem usually forming a short trunk, which sometimes grows to a height of fourteen foot. At the crown of the trunk long rigid leaves like coarse grass grow in a thick tuft and from that tuft an elongated flower stem emerges, reaching about six feet in length. After a bush fire, the blackened and charred remains of burnt trunks with the long flower stem, resemble a blackfellow carrying a spear; and suggest the name blackboy. The grass-trees are among the most notable Australian plants of ancient lineage.

Warwick, the second largest city of the Darling Downs, has a population of over 10,000. Its attractive setting on the banks of the Condamine River recalls the romantic bush ballad—the story in song of the loving Nancy pleading to her shearer sweetheart to be allowed to go with him:

'O Willy, dearest Willy, O let me go with you!
I'll cut off all my auburn fringe and be a shearer too;
I'll cook and count your tally, love, while ringer-o you shine,
And I'll wash your greasy moleskins on the banks of the
  Condamine . . .'

The Warwick district bred the first of Queensland's great
flocks of sheep, and today produces some of the finest wool and
grain in Australia. Timber, fruit, vegetables, cattle, pigs,
dairying and blood horses add to the wealth of this district.
Accommodation is taxed to its limit each October when
Warwick stages one of the State's main rodeos.

Killarney, 19 miles from Warwick, lies in a charming rural
setting of green hills and valleys on the southern edge of the
Darling Downs. Little wonder that the early settlers so named
it. Nearby are two National Parks in mountainous areas of the
Main Range. Here you encounter hardwood forests and a rain-
forest in a gorge where native birds are numerous and rock
wallabies and other marsupials abound.

Farther south is Stanthorpe and its Granite Belt, about 3,000
feet above sea-level, in the ranges near Queensland's southern
border. Stanthorpe is a flourishing fruit-growing area, producing applies, pears, plums, peaches and grapes; while fine
quality wool breeds on the surrounding grazing lands. An
Apple Blossom Festival is held each October. The wild flowers
around Stanthorpe are superb: there are some fifty species of
wattle, sixty species of native orchids, Flannel Flowers, Pink
Boronias, Flax lilies, Yellow Rock roses and Trigger-plants.

Whether one is a botanist or not, the trigger-plant must
amaze one. It is common enough throughout the land; yet few
people have studied its truly amazing performance. The
scientific name for this ancient plant is *Stylidium*, derived from
stylos, a column. It is easy to see how the plants got their
popular name, since a vital portion of the flower jerks up with
the unexpected suddenness of a trigger. These 'triggers' are so
delicately adjusted that the slightest touch is sufficient to shoot
off a million tiny granules of life. The beauty and efficiency of
the mechanism leaves one enthralled. Each of the trigger-plants
has its own peculiar manner of shooting; and though you have

watched them hundreds of times, the sudden spring of the trigger is always a surprising and delightful performance.

There are many unusual rock formations in the Granite Belt around Stanthorpe, including balancing rocks weathered by the ages. And if you are a 'rock hound' you will revel in the gem stones obtainable—topaz, crystal, amethyst, garnet and others.

Stanthorpe was originally called Quart Pot, after a local stream which is still known as Quart Pot Creek. When in 1870 the Government Surveyor altered the name of the town to its present one, the inhabitants strongly objected to the change, and meetings of protest were held. However, all objections were silenced when the Government Surveyor retorted: 'You must remember that this place may be a city some day, and there'll be a bishop here. It would never do if he had to sign himself, William, Bishop of Quart Pot!' That settled that. But so far Stanthorpe hasn't got its bishop.

FIVE

Lamington Plateau National Park

THIRTY miles east of Warwick, extending from Wilson's Peak (4,000 feet) to near Point Danger on the coast, is a spur of the Great Divide known as the McPherson Range. The Sydney-Brisbane coast railway crosses the range at Richmond Gap (part of the steep grade being negotiated by way of an unusual spiral tunnel) and the eastern part of the New South Wales and Queensland border runs along its ridge.

Much of the McPherson Range is volcanic in origin, heavily forested, very rugged, and affording some magnificent scenery, especially on the Lamington Plateau. The range was named by Allan Cunningham in 1828, after Major Duncan McPerson of the 39th Regiment. The town of Beaudesert, with a population of about 3,500, is the main centre of the Beaudesert Shire, which incorporates most of this region. Large areas of the shire have been reserved as National Parks for their natural beauty and verdant scrub lands.

The Lamington Plateau National Park comprises some 48,000 acres of jungle-clad gorges, tumbled mountains and ravines, giant cliffs, and many waterfalls. Geologists estimate that these mountains have been 18,000 to 20,000 feet high millions of years ago. Erosion by rain, wind, and heat has since worn them down to an average of 4,000 feet. Today the ancient vegetation survives—primitive mosses, unique orchids, avenues of fern trees, and creepers. The earliest mountain trees, beginning to grow in the shallow rock depressions left by the last great volcanic outburst, did not have enough soil to send down tap roots. So they grew buttresses, or thin sheet-like ribs, which extended about twelve feet from the central trunk and supplied food to the giants. They are still there. Ancient Antarctic beech-trees, which were standing fully grown a thousand years before Christ, are there.

Coomera Gorge, where a silver curtain of water plunges into a sunless pool at the bottom of the thousand-foot-deep gorge, is one of the most exciting places in the Lamington National Park: yet it is easy of access, and anybody who is prepared to walk four miles can enjoy it. In Spring the wildflowers and orchids are at their very best: Jasmine, Purple Sarsaparilla, White Clematis, Golden Sun Daisies, Snow Bush, Helesia, follow one another with a profusion of bloom and perfume. Mountain streams make music as they meander over boulders and dash in many cascades and falls made majestic by their height and volume.

Where jungles blocked the early explorers, you can now drive and walk, enjoying the wonders of nature. Bird life is abundant and here may be observed at close quarters the crimson rosella, the rufous scrub-bird, the Albert lyrebird, the golden regent, and satin bower-birds. These last are unique among the birds of the world; they construct a bower or playground leading to their nests and decorate it with as much colour as possible—preferring blue, to match their own glorious plumage. They like to use pieces of glass and bright tin, scraps of coloured paper, and gay flowers. Decoration is not done in a haphazard manner; a definite colour scheme and pattern is followed, and will be changed at various times according to mood.

An even more remarkable practice of the satin bower-bird is to 'paint' the inside of the bower, using dark-coloured fruits, charred wood and other vegetable matter, mixed with saliva. Consequently, although conceding that courtship and display are here the main purpose of the bower-bird, it has even been suggested that the practice of bower building has become a recreational pursuit and that the birds derive a certain aesthetic pleasure from their extraordinary building and decorative activities. The bower-birds (of which there are several species) were a source of amazement to the early naturalists. British naturalist John Gould wrote: 'Their highly decorated halls of assembly must be regarded as the most wonderful instances of bird architecture yet discovered.'

A lyrebird in full courting display is a sight to be remembered. The males have a gorgeous lyre-shaped tail, and during the breeding season build a series of cleared arenas in which they perform, like the peacock, the famous courting dance in which the splendid tail feathers are brought into play. The female is a small homely bird lacking any finery. The lyrebird—bird of a thousand voices—is unquestionably the prince of mocking birds. It mimics all bush noises. Frequently in the course of its own melodious song it will mimic the chopping of trees, sawing of logs, barking of dogs, clucking of hens or the laugh of a kookaburra, followed by the delightful clear notes of the thrush or magpie.

At Green Mountains, within the Lamington National Park, author Bernard O'Reilly, who has made this country familiar to many Australians, has a guest house which is run by the original pioneering family. Trips are arranged to see the many waterfalls, glow worms, look-outs and special scenic points. Guests on the lawn of the O'Reilly home feed not only the possums by hand, but also beautiful and often rare birds from the great forest. And at dusk wallabies come to be fed by the house, behind which is the nest of a bower-bird.

Green Mountains is especially rich in orchids; there are more than twenty species of ground, rock and tree orchids ranging from snowy-white to deep mauve. Here, too, are some of Queensland's loveliest trees—the flame tree, wheel of fire, tree waratahs and many others. But the park must be explored on foot, for there are no motorable roads beyond the guest-houses. There is, however an excellent network of walking tracks maintained by the sturdy axemen of Queensland's forest service. The axe no longer rings against lofty hoop pines, rosewood, rose mahogany and almonds; the men camp along the trails, keeping them free from fallen trees and other obstructions, and attending to camp-sites for visitors.

The Scrub turkeys in the sanctuary of the Green Mountains

are fairly plentiful. They do not sit on their eggs but bury them in incubation mounds. The mound is built by the male bird which has enormous toes for scratching and stamping building material of leaf mould, bush debris and soil. The Scrub turkey can build a mound up to five feet high and 20 feet across. He spends weeks and even months working on its construction. In fact, it can be said that his life is divided into three main phases —feeding, mound building and mound maintenance.

During building operations the male turkey will chase the hen away from the mound but let her climb on it to lay and bury her eggs. The male bird has his regular mound-duties to perform. He scratches the mound to let the sun warm it up: banks it up again to prevent over-heating. Thus the eggs are kept at an average temperature of about 90 degrees Fahrenheit, which suggests that the male Scrub turkey is equipped with a 'built-in thermometer'. On hatching, the chicks dig out of the mound and fend for themselves. Although these fascinating wild birds are always wary creatures, those in the Green Mountains are used to visitors, and have lost most of their shyness. The male wears a resplendent bright yellow wattle, but the hen's plumage is more conservative.

A ride on horseback through the luxuriant rain-forest is an unforgettable experience. Pathways follow rock pools and winding creeks into deep gorges and a world of cool green shadows. Lewin honey-eaters, blue-and-white wrens, and flights of crimson rosellas observe you on the way to one of the most beautiful of nature's gardens, where all is peace and loveliness in the misty wonder of the rain-forest.

Some of the mountain pools hold an unsolved mystery. Eels are found in them, but, apparently do not migrate to the sea, as other eels do. They could never climb up waterfalls more than 300 feet high in order to return to the Lamington Plateau, so evidently these unique eels spawn in their dwelling pools.

From one of the many scenic tracks one can see the highest peaks of the range, Mount Barney (4,450 feet) and Mount Lindesay (4,060 feet). The Glasshouse Mountains, a series of steep and massive pillars of trachyte, are also visible. These are among the most impressive geological formations in Australia, being volcanic survivals of the Cainozoic Age. The highest of the peaks is Mount Beerwah, an Aboriginal name meaning 'up in the sky'; and the mountain was always held in fear by the tribes who dwelt in the vicinity.

When John Petrie, one of the district's pioneers, announced his intention of climbing Beerwah, the Aborigines were terrified. Because of his understanding of them, he was much loved by the tribes. They implored him not to make the ascent, saying that a great Spirit dwelt on the summit of the mountain, and would punish with blindness anyone daring to look at him. They assured Petrie that only once had the peak been climbed and that, sure enough, the foolish native who accomplished it had been struck blind.

John laughed at their superstition, and said that a white man need have no such fears. He ascended the peak; but shortly afterwards, by an extraordinary coincidence, became totally and permanently blind.

Just north of the McPherson Range rises the scarp of the outlying Tamborine Mountain, a splendid plateau eight miles long and up to four miles wide, and curved like a great boomerang. Tamborine Mountain, named from the Aboriginal term 'Tehembrin', or 'the wild lime tree', is a serene, evergreen place where the silence is seldom broken save for the sound of cascading water, and the cries of the bell and whip bird and of the vari-coloured parikeets and lorikeets.

Witches' Falls Park, on Tamborine Mountain, was the first National Park area set aside for the people in Queensland; and other territory on the mountain has been added since. From the village of Tamborine a road leads up the mountain as far as Curtis Falls, and there forks left to Eagle Heights and right to North Tamborine and St Bernards. The Eagle Heights settlement overlooks a spectacular view of the coast, stretching from Moreton Bay southward to beyond Point Danger, and across the blue foothills of the McPherson Range and the Springbrook and Tamborine plateaus.

At Eagle Heights, beyond an area which looks out over the forest towards the sea, graded paths lead down into the Palm Grove. This is a sheltered pocket of rain-forest and of piccabeen palms, a tall species with feathery leaves, also known as the bangalow palm. The spathes of the piccabeen were used by the

Aborigines for water-containers. Here are some of the most remarkable trees on Mount Tamborine: great figs whose age can only be guessed at; and carrabeens, their extraordinary, high buttress roots green with mosses and creeping ferns.

Easy paths beckon the bushwalker through the forest to waterfalls and look-outs. There is continual interest on the way: caves, giant trees, miniature orchids, delicate hares' foot fern, and mosses; shy bush animals and birds. Little dark rock wallabies hop across the bush paths, and where vines and tree-orchids flower overhead, the boom of the great purple-breasted pigeon is heard and the squeaking and quarreling of a flying-fox camp. The paths in certain seasons are strewn with the red bell flowers of the flame trees, one of the glories of the rain-forest; and with the crimson spokes of the Wheel of Fire tree, and the red and yellow flowers of the black-bean or Moreton Bay chestnut tree. Tangles of lianas and pepper vine hang from the tall branches, and the ever-present staghorns, elk-horns and other epiphytes cling to the trunks and boughs high above. Out in the open forest you are sure to glimpse families of blue or red-backed wrens, or flights of brilliant parakeets on their way home from one feeding ground to another.

Tamborine is famous for its variety of butterflies, some of which breed only on certain rain-forest plants and are rare elsewhere. Few people realize that Australia possesses about 340 species of butterflies, many of which are highly perfumed. Some exhale a flower-like odour linking them with the blossoms they frequent. It seems quite certain that these perfumes are used as an adjunct in courtship. The skippers, so called because of their skipping manner of flight, comprise more than a quarter of the butterflies of Australia. The regent skipper is one of the most admired of this species owing to its vivid colouring—black with glass-like golden spots and green markings beneath. The larger varieties of the regent skipper have brilliant fiery eyes. Treasured by collectors are the scintillating swallow-tails of the north and the exquisite *Delias*, the largest of this species being confined to south-eastern Australia. The *Delias* have bright yellow splashes with a band of broad scarlet spots. Unrivalled for brilliancy of blues and greens and purples are the *Ogyris* of northern Australia.

Drilling for oil at Roma, Queensland, early this century (page 27)

The oil bore fire controlled (page 27)

Stoney Creek Falls in flood, North Queensland   (page 13)

Favourites, too, are the dainty and beautiful *Lycaenidae*—
blues, coppers and hairstreaks.

On the northern side of Eagle Heights is Macdonald Park, the
western side of which looks across the Logan Valley to the
Limestone Hills of Ipswich and the Bremer and Brisbane
Valleys. From the vantage point of the Knoll area there is a
richly rewarding walk through a particularly beautiful part of
the forest to Cameron Falls.

Along the Western Cliff Road to the St Bernard Hotel there
are extensive views of the Canungra Valley and the crests of the
McPherson Range. The hotel has the distinction of being
built 'round a macrozamia palm tree, which scientists estimate
to be over 10,000 years old'. The swimming pool is fed by a
natural spring among tall eucalypts and tree-ferns, and the
hotel's ten acres of parklands—where the avocado pear thrives
—have a floral display that delights gardeners. Beyond the
hotel a road leads to the south eastern face of the mountain
with panoramic views down the coast past the New South
Wales border and northward beyond Moreton Bay. The
Coomera Valley lies below, and mountains of the border range,
with their foothills crowding the cliffs of Tamborine, show
patches of green clearing which include the peaceful pastures
of the Beechmont and Springbrook plateaus.

Off the main road is the Macrozamia Park reserve, the
western slope of which is heavily clothed with the extraordinary
macrozamia palms. Those in the reserve—they grow at their
best on Tamborine—include several of the oldest palms extant.
There are conflicting estimates of the age of these cycads, but
whatever it is the species is of very ancient lineage, going back
millions of years to the Coal Age era.

Throughout Australia there are a considerable number of
reservations which are known variously as national parks,
national forests, national reserves, sight reserves, faunal reserves,
and sanctuaries. The last name is applied more specifically to
areas which are reservations only in the sense that interference
with fauna or flora is prohibited. The most significant of the
reservations, in general, are the national parks, such as these
of Queensland with their assertive grandeur of mountain and

gorge; they are for the most part primitive or semi-primitive areas dedicated to the public, and preserved, as far as may be, in their natural conditions. In the course of time they will become more and more a precious heritage.

Legally, there is no national park in New South Wales. Reservations to which the term is applied are created simply by governmental proclamations, and it is possible for them to be decreased in size or otherwise subjected to interference at the whims of governments. Perish the thought.

SIX

Spoilers of the Forest

FROM the McPherson Range to the Northern Rivers of New South Wales, and extending almost to the sea, hundreds of square miles of great hardwood forest country was once known as the Big Scrub. The scrub was of such a mass, and composed of such variety of giant timber, that it is difficult to imagine its grandeur and beauty. Cedar and fig, bean and beech, pine and stinging nettle, rosewood and cudgery, teak and blackapple, and many other varieties of trees, some extremely valuable, others commercially valueless, struggled together for existence. In the struggle their leaves intermingled, forming a dense shade, so that no direct sunlight reached the ground below. This was continually damp, and always thickly covered with leaves.

The scrub contained, too, a great variety of orchids, many mosses, and birds' nest and staghorn ferns. The trees were bound together with great vines like ships' cables, beautiful lawyer vines and others also forming an impassable barrier. Many of the scrub trees yielded fruit, and were visited by a great variety of birds. The soil of the Big Scrub country is decomposed basalt, red in colour, containing much red iron oxide, extremely loose when dry, and very deep. Before the days of settlement, however, the scrub was seldom, if ever, dry. The hardy early pioneers elected to go into this trackless region, where bounteous rains, fertile soil and a sub-tropical climate combined to produce a vegetable growth of great abundance and luxuriance. To bring this under cultivation was the difficulty; but they knew that they had to face privations and difficulties, and were not to be deterred.

One of the pioneers said that the Aborigines of the district—men, women, boys and girls—were expert tree climbers. In climbing, they made use of a vine about three-quarters of an inch thick. 'This was passed around the tree trunk, and the two ends grasped by the climber, one in either hand, a loop at one extremity for the purpose of giving a slight foothold, while the other was in the step cut through the bark, and portion of the sap, with a tomahawk. These steps were about seven or eight feet apart, and formed but a precarious rest for the side of the foot close to the small toe, thus bearing the full weight of the body. By holding the ends of the vine, and pressing his foot against the barrel, the climber advanced by a series of steps, jerking the vine upwards as he ascended till the next step was reached. These notches were cut by the right hand about 15 inches above the head, while both ends of the vine were held in the left hand, and the other foot lightly supported by the loop.'

Another pioneer settler said that it was the custom of the Aborigines of the district to scarify the body of a youth when he became a man. To prepare for this 'He immersed himself in the cold water of a creek (generally in the winter time), and, upon coming out, he was held down by several other men while others beat his chest with nettles, and then one took a sharp flint and drew it across the youth's chest inflicting a deep cut. He was then removed to a fire where the wound was dried. But, until it was quite healed, he was not allowed to converse with anybody.'

The Aborigines made no attempt to cultivate the soil and grow their own food materials. They were hunters and fishers. Here they found plenty of game—kangaroos, wallabies, bandicoots, possums, snakes, fishes, wild ducks, swans, and very many other varieties of game. Fights between the different tribes were frequent. A pioneer thus describes a typical battle:

'In preparing for these fights the warriors smeared their bodies with grease and burnt stringy bark, and then painted fanciful or extraordinary patterns with ochre coloured clay. Their woolly hair was ruffled and expanded to its fullest extent so as to make the face appear small. Sometimes the hair was speckled with a mixture of swan down and cockatoo's feathers. A favourite adornment of the face was an ochre stripe—about one and a half inches long across the small of the nose and the cheeks.

'The only uniform was a belt or girdle round the loins which carried boomerang and paddy-melon stick, the spear and shields engaging the hands as the attacker advanced. The shield was about 18 inches long and 10 inches wide.

'Armed thus the natives approached one another, yelling their war cries while the older men and women folk looked on out of range and "barracked" with all their might. Spears, boomerangs and paddy sticks went flying with deadly precision, but they were generally turned aside by the expert use of the shield. When a man was wounded he retired to where the women and old men were. There the wound was sucked vigorously till the blood ceased to flow, and the warrior rushed once more into the fray.'

The little border township of Limpinwood in the McPherson Range commemorates an old-timer known as 'Hopping Dick' Wood. He was a timber cutter in the days when pine and cedar logs were hauled by bullock teams to Murwillumbah and shipped to Sydney. Dick had suffered a broken leg which, due to lack of medical attention, had mended shorter than the other, giving him the nickname of Hopping Dick. Along a stream now known as Hopping Dick Creek he discovered a forest of valuable red and white cedar. Here he blazed a trail where the timber-getters fought their way through the virgin rain-forests, hauling the giant logs all the way to Murwillumbah. Dick Wood and his helpers took out all the cedar, except for a few trees growing on inaccessible precipices of the mountains.

Although here as elsewhere the magnificent red cedar country was depleted by these spoilers of the forest, it must be admitted that the cedar-getters played an important part in the development of the States. They were pioneers of pioneers, preceding the settlers. When what is now known as Limpinwood was thrown open for settlement at the turn of the century, it was called Hopping Dick Creek. A bark and slab schoolhouse was opened in that name; but the settlers soon decided to change the name of the new district. They were unanimous in calling the settlement Limping Wood, while retaining the name Hopping Dick for the creek. This was eventually standardized as 'Limpinwood', and has remained so ever since.

Hopping Dick was the inspiration for a ballad which was composed by one of the original settlers:

> 'Did you ever hear of Hopping Dick,
>   a settler of the Tweed
> A man who faced the lonely bush,
>   when all was wild indeed?
> When scrub was dense, and the woodman's axe
>   resounded from afar;
> And the dingo's howl came through the night,
>   before talk of Murwillumbah.
> When money made was freely spent
>   on stronger stuff than water;
> They were devil-me-care these settler men,
>   though of course, they "shouldn't oughter."
> But cedar and pine brought them gold,
>   'twas easy come and go;
> And such were the lives of many men
>   who are now laid below.
> And one of these was Hopping Dick,
>   whose memory survives
> In the name of a creek, where settlers thick
>   are living out their lives.
> And down the stream a mound now marks
>   the grave of this sturdy man;
> One who was brave and fought the bush,
>   and therein lived life's span.'

Since the beginning of the nineteenth century, the Hawkesbury, the Hunter, the Illawarra, and the Shoalhaven districts of New South Wales had been continuously exploited for the splendid red cedar (*Cedrela australis*) abounding in the river valleys and the ranges thereabout. By the 1850s this valuable timber was wiped out, but with the discovery of the magnificent red cedar country of the Northern Rivers the cedar-getters turned their attention to the rich new field.

Though most of these men were wild and irresponsible they had a rough code of law governing their operations, one canon of which was that no pair of sawyers could claim a right to more trees than they could saw at one pit.

The first export of Australian cedar was made in 1795 when the vessel *Experiment* took some of the timber to India. David Smith, one of the early cedar-getters of the Illawarra district, stated that there was scarcely a valley, ravine or gorge of the south coast that was not dotted with cedar trees. Governor Macquarie had one noble tree measured during his visit to the district in 1820; it was 100 feet high and 21 feet in circumference 10 feet from the base. (The red cedar, which is indigenous to Australia, reaches a height of about 150 feet.)

In July 1799, Captain Flinders was sent in the *Norfolk* to examine the coast of New South Wales, north of Sydney, particularly those parts passed by Captain Cook in the night time. (From 1788 to 1859 Queensland was included in the then colony of New South Wales.) Flinders was also on the lookout for some large river which might lead into the heart of Australia. He discovered and named Shoal Bay, but was disappointed to find no indication of the big river of which he was in search. Had he made a closer examination of the country which, according to his journal, did not seem to show 'anything of particular interest', he would have glimpsed the wonderful cedar forests that encircled the Northern Rivers districts.

The first white men to see the cedar forests of the North were seven convicts, escapees from the Moreton Bay penal settlement. They had wandered for six years with a tribe of Aborigines. One of the convicts, a man named Craig, learned in 1834 that a free pardon was offered to any convict who discovered some bullocks that had strayed from the settlement at Moreton Bay. Craig found them, delivered them to the authorities, and claimed and got his freedom. He reported that during his walkabouts with the Aborigines he had seen a river a mile wide, around which there was much land suited for pasturage, while all about were 'beautiful cedar trees'.

A century ago the Clarence, Richmond, Tweed, Dorrigo and Brunswick rivers of this region had their banks lined with towering trees in areas of hundreds of square miles of great hardwood forest. There was an astonishing variety of timbers, including red cedar, beech, pine, rosewood, teak, bean and cudgery. The forests, too, were the haunts of many species of birds such as the bronzewing and wonga pigeons, regent birds, satin birds and rifle birds. Especially beautiful was the regent bird with its brilliant orange and black plumage; but even more striking was the rifle bird with its shot plumage of purple and black and scale-like feathers of green and gold.

Until 1836 Sydney timber merchants were getting all their cedar supplies from the Illawarra and other southern areas; but now there was a great demand for the red cedar of the North. Soon after Craig's disclosure of cedar country in this newly-discovered region, both cedar-getters and squatters made haste there. The squatters could occupy the land on payment of a license fee of £10 a year, and timber-getters were allowed to cut trees on payment of a license of £6 a year for cedar and £2 a year for hardwood. If a man held the two licenses he could cut any timber.

The first sawyers to enter the red cedar trade established their camp on a site which is now part of the town of Maclean. Here was a wonderful growth of red cedar right on the river banks. After felling, all the cedar-getters had to do was to make cross cuts, roll the logs into the river, and float them down stream.

News of the new cedar land spread rapidly and soon bands of sawyers from the Illawarra and other districts were making their way north to seek their fortunes. The cedar-getters were like prospectors in search of goldfields. They discovered abundance of cedar in one find after another, and new rushes set in along the Richmond, the Clarence, the Brunswick and the Tweed districts. They always worked in groups and found it convenient, while working on the river banks, to live in their whale boats, and move these homes up and down the river as required. Their licenses permitted them to build huts but not to cultivate land, or buy it. This was one of the reasons why the sawyers lived a wild, irresponsible existence.

Alexander Harris, an emigrant mechanic, writing the story of his colonial experiences under the title of *Settlers and Convicts*, relates an experience with the cedar-getters, when he and his mate were camped near them in about 1825.

The colours of the Cooktown orchid vary according to the different plants, the majority being deep purple   (page 7)

Bunyip drawn by an Aboriginal in the Lake Bathurst district, New South Wales   (page 29)

Bunyip as depicted by an Aboriginal of the Murray River in 1848   (page 29)

Coomera Falls, in the McPherson Range National Park
(page 36)

'. . . At first we did not much heed the shouting and shrieking in every tone and dialect, from that of cockneyism to that of the Irish province which is said to be a mile beyond his Satanic Majesty's residence; but it came nearer and nearer. At last it crossed the river, and came up the road through the bush; and by the time we were out at the fire in our shirts, the whole corps debouched before us. Some wore check shirts, some wore woollen; some were in red ones and some in blue, and some in none at all; some had straw hats, some Scotch caps, some old working skull-caps, some nothing but their own shock heads of hair; some had sticks in their hands, some the ration-bags they had been to get filled; some the axe they had been sharpening at the grindstone and some three or four ribs of salted beef for tomorrow's dinner; some sang, some yelled, some said nothing, but the one unanimous demand was the remainder of our stock of rum.

'All remonstrances were ineffectual. I was told at last that if I did not give it they would take it, and put me on the fire for a back-log. Of course, further parley was useless; I brought it out, and they set to at it with all the pannikins they could muster . . .' Elsewhere he says 'a more unlicensed and reckless mob . . . prolonging day into night in their carousal until all the liquor was gone, it would be impossible to find anywhere'.

John Henderson (*Excursions and Adventures in New South Wales*, 1851) describes the cedar-getters in general as a strange set; they were mostly desperate ruffians, often ticket-of-leave men or emancipists, and sometimes runaways. 'They labour very hard but they are certainly the most improvident set of men in the world, often eclipsing in recklessness, misery and peculiarity of character the woodcutters of Campeachy and the lumberers of the Ohio and Mississippi.'

A newspaper report of the late 1860s refers to the sawyer as 'the roughest of rough fellows, muscular as a working bullock, hairy as a chimpanzee, obstinate as a mule, simple as a child, generous as the slave of Aladdin's lamp'. Adding that characteristics of the men included a fondness for rum-drinking and a weakness for fighting, the writer concludes: 'There is a good deal of rude honour about these fellows. Thus, if one chance to

The Barron Falls, near Cairns, North Queensland   (page 13)

light upon a "fall" of cedar, none of the others will attempt to cut even a tree out of the group'.

The Reverend Dr. Lang, writing of conditions in the timber country in 1856, said that the cedar-getters 'were denied every opportunity of making homes for themselves and were driven perforce to spend their evenings in riotous dissipation and reduce their wives and families to misery and ruin'. He mentions one case where a cedar-getter had saved £800, and then, the squatter on whose run he had erected his hut having threatened to evict him for trespass, 'had so lost heart that he spent the whole lot in one frenzied dissipation'.

It became the custom of the cedar-getters to hand their money over to the store-keeper, rum seller, or later to the hotel-keeper to hold, and when it was all spent to go out and cut down more timber. No school was built in the Northern Rivers districts for many years after the first settlements; nor were there resident clergymen or doctors. Most of the squatters' children received their education at home, but those of the cedar-getters generally grew up in ignorance. The food of these people was of the simplest kind—usually corned beef, damper and tea—but often the little schooners that brought the supplies would be bar-bound and there would be a severe shortage of foodstuffs.

The winning of the cedar was no easy task. Little difficulty was experienced with the trees on the rivers' edges, but when these were depleted the sawyers had to fight their way through the scrubs and forests to get at the prized cedars. When the trees were felled they were cross-cut into logs which were branded so that the owners could distinguish them. To get the logs down to some stream which, when flooded, would carry them down to the river, necessitated the cutting of a track through the scrub and the employment of bullocks. The cedar-getters continued with their cutting till the heavy rains came; then all hands set to work to put the logs into the raging torrent. The red logs rushed down the various swollen streams till they reached the river, where they were caught in hundreds by chains stretched across their track. When the flood had abated, the logs of each owner were sorted and made into rafts. Logs which could not be sent down to the rivers were chopped into flitches and hauled to market by bullock teams.

Some of the cedar trees yielded immense quantities of timber, a good tree containing about 25,000 feet, and one red cedar felled at Booyong yielding 33,000 feet. Even in those days cedar was worth £1 a hundred feet. As the forests and scrubs became denuded of this wealth of timber, the sawyers turned their attention to the abundance of pine and various hardwoods. According to the *Report of the Intercolonial Exhibition of 1870* at Sydney, no less than 3,639,933 super feet of cedar was sent to Sydney in 1869 alone. The figure for pine and ash sent to Sydney in the same year was 5,567,250 feet.

So ruthlessly were these magnificent timbers stripped that little was left at the dawn of the present century. Today— except in some of the National Parks—the great forests are no more. Settlers seeking land for sugar-cane or dairying destroyed many millions of feet of extremely valuable timbers— the red cedar, beech, bean, rosewood and teak. The timber could not be used at anything like the rate at which it was being cut down, and so the trees had to be burned where they lay. Never again will Australia see the grandeur and beauty of the great red cedar country that was once part of her heritage.

SEVEN

New England

FROM the Queensland border to the Moonbi Range in New South Wales, with the North Coast district on the east of it, and the North-west Slopes on the west, lies the plateau of New England. This extensive but undefined area of New South Wales is the largest region of highland in Australia. The plateau—some 9,000 square miles in area—has an altitude of more than 3,000 feet and its main peaks are 5,000 feet, and higher. They include the Round Mountain (5,300 feet), Point Lookout (5,250 feet), Mount Bajimba (5,000 feet), and Ben Lomond where the highest railway station in Australia is located. On the eastern side, the plateau drops rapidly from 5,000 feet to the coastal plains by way of a zone of canyons separated by steep ridges which gradually flatten towards the coast.

The history of New England dates from 1818, when explorer John Oxley and his party crossed the southern end of the tableland on their journey eastwards from the Macquarie River to Port Macquarie on the coast. The first occupant of the territory is believed to have been H. C. Sempill of Belltrees, Scone, who, in 1832, established a station property which he named Wolka. Today it is the site of the township of Walcha.

Early settlers in one part of the New England area headed their letters 'New Caledonia'. To the Aborigines it was known as Arrabald. By 1837 about thirty squatters had sent their flocks and herds to the district, and it was about this time that the name 'New England' appeared and has been used ever since. John Henderson, in his *Excursions and Adventures in New South Wales*, published in 1851, described New England as follows:

'New England is studded with stations at the distance of ten and fifteen miles from each other, and is chiefly, or entirely, occupied by young gentlemen of respectability and education, who have emigrated from Great Britain. In this respect it is much superior to Liverpool Plains, the stations in which, for the most part, belong to old-established settlers, who live within the bounds of the colony, and leave their establishments in the interior to be managed by super-intendents and overseers often procured from the lower or emancipated orders.

'Within the last two years, one or two ladies have found their way into the New England district, which was formerly inhabited by young bachelors exclusively; and when wives can be found for more of them and their men, the comfort of the stations and the respectability of the district will be much increased.'

One of the notorious bushrangers who roved the New England country was Wilson, who was ultimately captured. Two days after he had been executed, with his lieutenant, Long Tom, at Maitland, a free pardon arrived for him from England. It is claimed that the bushranger was the natural son of an English baronet.

Because of their geographical position, the people of New England are strongly in favour of being part of a new State which would incorporate a greater area than the name implies. The Constitution of the Commonwealth of Australia provides machinery for the creation of new States by the granting of self-government to Federal Territories; by the subdividing of existing States; or by the union of parts of States. At a New England referendum held in 1967, however, many of the people of the extended area, were not in favour of a new State, and defeated the issue.

The chief industries of New England are agriculture, grazing, orcharding and vegetable-growing. Merino wool is produced, and cattle-breeding is also an important occupation in certain areas. The cool upland climate is suitable for stone and pome fruits and for potatoes, great quantities of which are sent to the Sydney market.

The city of Armidale and the towns of Glen Innes, Walcha, Uralla, Tenterfield and Guyra are the main centres of population. The early settlers along the northern rivers of New South Wales had two routes by which they could reach New England. One led from South Grafton over the Macleay Range to the Guyra and Armidale district, and the other was from Grafton through Lawrence, Wyan and Tabulam to Tenterfield. Travelling by the latter route—considered the better of the two—took twelve days in fine weather, and several weeks in wet. The journey to Armidale in the 1860s could be done by bullock dray in sixteen days in dry weather. Some of the Armidale folk, impatient at the slow progress of the railway from Morpeth, were urging better roads and even railway communication between Grafton and Armidale, with improvements to the Clarence so that the river could be their port. At the same time the Clarence River folk were urging the making of a good road to Tenterfield and other New England areas.

The results were improvements to the old route, which was renamed the New Road. This and other roads to New England brought a great amount of trade to the Clarence, first by bullock team, then by horse team. These links between the North Coast and the New England tableland traverse some of the steepest country in New South Wales and are indicative of the fact that the fast-flowing coastal rivers were greater barriers to roadmaking than were the precipitous mountain slopes of the Great Dividing Range. The construction of the New England railway in the 'eighties caused most of the trade to disappear.

It was during an inspection of one of the old bullock tracks that went round the head of the Tuckianne Swamp, about 15 miles south of Lismore, that I met our old friend the bunyip. An old-timer told me that the early settlers were afraid to go near the swamp because of the presence of a bunyip there; moreover he remembered all the lines of a ballad concerning it. This quaint piece of Australian mythology—written a century or more ago—is well worthy to go on record. To be sure, the rustic recitations that charmed our forefathers are often crude

and worthless verse, but they give us a picture of life in early
colonial days as seen through the eyes of the ordinary man—
the drover, the digger, the shearer, the newly-arrived immi-
grant. We must remember that they were composed when the
population was a curious conglomeration of highly-educated
and ignorant people. Books and papers were luxuries, so
ballad-making came into vogue just as it had done in Europe
centuries before.

> Far off in lonely Tuckianne Swamp the
>   awful Bunyip cries;
> His home is in the tall green reeds
>   where deep the water lies.
> There, safe among the shady trees,
>   beneath the verdant mud,
> He sleeps all day and wakes at night
>   to gambol in the flood.
> His body's like a yearling colt; his claws
>   are sharp and strong;
> His tail is like a rough pine log some
>   nine or ten feet long;
> His head is long, his neck is thick,
>   with a long, waving mane,
> And those who ever saw him once ne'er
>   wish to look again.
> His voice is that of mountain bulls—it
>   echoes through the trees,
> And rolls around the dismal swamp,
>   borne on the midnight breeze;
> But those who dwell near Tuckianne Swamp
>   well know the dreadful sound
> The Bunyip makes when he comes out
>   and walks upon the ground.
> There is an ancient prophecy (how true
>   I cannot say)
> That says that he will ne'er be caught
>   until there comes a day
> When ladies three shall go for him and
>   shall not be afraid,

> And one shall be a widow, one a matron,
>   one a maid.
> And when that day shall come to pass
>   without the help of man,
> The Bunyip shall no more be heard in
>   lonely Tuckianne.

Whether the bunyip was ever laid by the means the ballad suggests, my informant could not say. In Tuckianne Swamp, however, he showed me the nest of the jabiru, a stately bird that frequents swamps and lagoons. The jabiru is the only bird in the world incapable of uttering a cry, and the Aboriginal legend telling why he is dumb is a quaint and delightful one:

There was a time when the jabiru was not only a very garrulous bird but a real old nosey. He just could not keep out of other people's affairs, and went about chuckling and prattling like a gossiping old woman. Now, as most people know, the Aboriginal initiation rites are always held in strict secrecy; no woman is ever allowed to be present. Well, this particular old busybody of a jabiru hid himself in a tree above the bora ground, watched the proceedings, and subsequently told two lubras all about what took place at the ceremony. They in turn, like some others of their sex, could not keep the information to themselves, and soon all the women of the tribe had heard about the secrets.

The men were furious, so they captured the bird and sentenced it to have its tongue bitten off by a carpet snake. When the reptile came to do his job he pretended that he wanted to have a look inside the jabiru's fine long beak. However, the wily old bird had his revenge on the cunning snake. Though the latter bit off the jabiru's tongue, the bird shut down his great beak with a terrible smack on the reptile's head. That is why all carpet snakes have flat heads, and why the jabirus are known as the birds of silence.

The 56,000-acre New England National Park attracts many visitors; mountain walks lead into forest and scrub where fast-flowing streams tumble through gorges, spilling over cascades and waterfalls. Point Lookout provides probably the most extensive panorama of mountain, valley and coastal country of any point on the Great Dividing Range. Despite its altitude,

Fred Ward, better known as 'Thunderbolt' (page 58)

The disfigured Thunderbolt's Rock; the bushranger's hideout (page 58)

The Jabiru, the bird of silence   (page 56)

A convict-built road, near Glen Innes, New South Wales (page 61)

much of New England is admirably suited for agriculture. The rich soils of the plateau receive more than thirty inches of rain annually and have been intensively cultivated, especially around the main centres.

The countryside is at its best from September to Christmas with mile upon mile of burgeoning apple and cherry orchards; acres of maize, peas, potatoes and cabbages thriving in the spring sunshine; sheep grazing in the pastures. But it is in Autumn that New England lives up to its name. The pioneers nostalgically planted their new gardens and roadsides with thousands of deciduous trees from England, and in March and April streets and parks glow with the russet-gold leaves from poplar and silver birch, pine, oak and claret ash.

The old mining settlement of Hillgrove is worth visiting. This, together with Rocky River, was at one time 'gold-rush' country, 92,000 ounces of gold being won in a single year. Today holiday 'prospectors' are frequently seen camped along the banks of the rivers in search of the elusive yellow metal. Of more lasting importance was the discovery of tin last century, tin mining still being an important source of New England income. Much hidden treasure, too, may be found in the way of gemstones, including sapphires, emeralds, amethysts, garnets, topaz, zircons and industrial diamonds.

Armidale, the 'capital' of New England and the only city in the region, is a noted ecclesiastical and educational centre. It has two cathedrals, a university, and a teachers' college, as well as major schools and colleges. The renowned Hinton Benefaction Art Gallery contains the most valuable art collection of any country gallery in the Commonwealth. In the grounds of the Teachers' College is the Educational Museum, where a mid-Victorian Standard School from a bush hamlet has been re-erected and equipped with the teaching devices and furniture of that era. Interesting, too, is a folk museum portraying the life of ordinary New England people of the past.

One of Armidale's thoroughfares is called Beardy Street, named after two pioneering characters. 'The Beardies' were well-known stockmen so nicknamed because of the long, black beards they wore. In the early days of settlement when men used to arrive from Sydney looking for suitable land and livestock, they were always advised to consult the Beardies, who had a thorough knowledge of the pastoral country. Their names were Duval and Chandler, and they are commemorated, also, in the naming of Beardy Waters and Beardy River. Another tribute was paid them in 1922 when a New England municipality brought out a publication entitled *The Land of the Beardies*, to mark its jubilee.

The mountainous district around Armidale abounds with interest for the nature lover, and the many streams are a magnet for the trout fisherman. A trout hatchery has been established on the Serpentine River and is open for inspection. One of the prettiest drives in the district is along the Arding Lanes, which meander through the fruit-growing country between Armidale and Uralla, via Rocky River. The town of Uralla, with its golden poplars, bird haven lagoons and old-world touches, holds much charm for the visitor. The district is given over mainly to the production of fine Merino wool, fat lambs and cattle raising. Cold-climate fruits, oats and potatoes are also grown.

It is in the Uralla cemetery that the legendary bushranger of New England, Frederick Ward, is buried. His grave is well tended and flowers are still often placed upon it. Many people visit the outlaw's last resting place, which is marked by a headstone erected and kept in order by New England residents.

This bushranger, better known as 'Thunderbolt', had a favourite haunt near Uralla, from which to spot approaching police; this is known as Thunderbolt's Rock. The last of the bushrangers in New South Wales, he commenced his reign in 1863, holding up coach after coach. But he never used violence. Many were his daring robberies, and invariably this good-looking outlaw would ride away with his plunder, singing at the top of his voice. Although wanted dead or alive (and he was finally shot down in 1870) the troubadour bushranger inspired none of the terror caused by some of the early outlaws. Indeed his exploits were taken good-humouredly by most people, for he had lots of friends and admirers.

A tale is told that Thunderbolt held up a German brass band while the musicians were rehearsing in the district of Goonoo Goonoo, on their way to the town of Tenterfield. When the conductor of the band protested that they would be stranded without the few pounds that they possessed, Thunderbolt said he was sorry but that he wanted to put the money on a 'dead cert' at the Tenterfield races the following day. He added, however, that if the horse won he would return the money in care of the Tenterfield post-office. Thunderbolt's horse won his race, and the money was returned to the German band.

On one occasion Thunderbolt rode up to Tabulam Station, on the Clarence River. He was picturesquely dressed in a cabbage-tree hat, moleskins and a blue shirt. Nearing the homestead he dismounted and tied up his thoroughbred horse. The lady of the household was not unduly alarmed at the sight of the handsome stranger, who flourished his hat and asked politely, 'May I crave a glass of water?' She fetched him the water and, as he drank, he remarked casually, 'You are alone, I presume?' 'Yes', she answered, guilelessly. The gallant stranger then blew a whistle and two other men appeared from nowhere. The lady was wearing a beautiful enamelled watch suspended round her neck. (This watch was given at her death to the Sydney Art Gallery.) When Thunderbolt demanded it she said that it had belonged to her dear mother and was the only keepsake she had of her. 'You can keep it,' Thunderbolt replied, 'but lead us over the house. We want all the money and valuables you have.'

As the owner of the house had taken everything of value into Casino that morning, the lady did not mind showing them over the place, where they found nothing to their purpose. As they passed one of the bedrooms she turned to Thunderbolt, saying, 'Will you please tell them to walk on tiptoe past this door? My sister is ill and must not be disturbed.' Then followed the strange sight of the crinolined lady with three bushrangers in her wake all walking on tiptoe.

Australian history would be less fascinating without these plundering sons, and Australian art—from Tom Roberts to Sidney Nolan—would be poorer. Sinners they were; but they repaid their society richly with story and legend.

One of the highest towns in New South Wales is named Guyra: an Aboriginal word meaning 'fish may be caught', and apt for a district where there is splendid fishing in the local streams, particularly for trout and eels. Many balancing rock formations are found in this part of New England, two of the most unusual being the Mushroom Rock and the Haystack. The Mushroom is a series of three rocks, the top one, which is the largest, resembling a giant mushroom; the Haystack is a large single granite boulder, 70 yards around the base and 30 feet high.

Guyra made headline news in 1921 when its invisible poltergeist manifested itself, becoming one of the most inexplicable and well-attested of Australian ghosts. For about a month the household of a local council worker suffered almost nightly disturbances, seeming to have a ghostly origin. Stones were thrown through windows; the walls of the cottage rocked as if under sledge-hammer blows. Police and volunteers by the score kept nightly watch. The attacks continued, seemingly without human agency.

For a while suspicion fell on the 12-year-old daughter of the house. It was soon obvious, however, that she was guiltless, for the attacks continued while she was under observation. After a month, quiet again descended on the house. Psychic researchers were convinced a poltergeist was responsible. No other satisfactory explanation could be offered by the police or anyone else—either for the attacks on the house or for the mysterious vanishing at the time of an 87-year-old Irishwoman, Mrs Doran, who was never seen again.

Of all Australian hauntings, none caused greater argument and discussion than the affair at Guyra. The ghost cottage still stands in the town.

Most southerly of the main New England centres is Walcha, on the Apsley River, near the spot where the explorer John Oxley camped on his 1818 expedition of discovery. It was here that aerial agriculture in Australia was first introduced. The Tiger Moth plane used in the first dusting operations is preserved in the grounds of the Pioneer Cottage, a folk museum furnished in the style of a typical pioneer home and maintained by the Walcha Historical Society. Walcha, named from an Aboriginal word meaning 'sun', is a favourite place for sportsmen, having wild pig and duck shooting and, as elsewhere in New England, many miles of trout streams.

Glen Innes is a town of pleasant parks and tree-lined streets. Conditions here are ideal for horticulture, dahlias and roses growing to perfection. Rose Festival Week, held around October to November, is a good time to appreciate the beauty of Glen Innes, when myriads of flowers are in bloom. The surrounding countryside of pastures, hills and valleys adds to one's pleasure. To the east, the Gwydir Highway crosses the Gibraltar Range, where sheer escarpments, deep-carved river valleys and high rain-forests invite a walkabout.

Sapphire mining is carried out on a fairly extensive scale in the district, while lots of residents and visitors fossick as a hobby. Not surprisingly, a local mineral and gem club is active. Other minerals being worked are tin and bismuth: it was from a local mine that the largest slug of bismuth ever found in Australia was recovered. Glen Innes honours the name of Major Archibald Clune Innes, a Scotsman, who was one of the first settlers in New England.

Inverell, another thriving town in the region, is named after a property of that name which covered 50,000 acres along the Macintyre River. The owner, a certain Alexander Campbell, was inspired to call it thus because of the many wild swans he saw on the river; Inverell is Gaelic for 'meeting place of the swan'. Besides being richly productive agriculturally, the Inverell district has a wealth of varied mineral resources, the principal minerals being tin, sapphires, zircons and industrial diamonds. More of these last are found here than in any other part of Australia. There are deposits, also, of silver, bauxite, coal, limestone and phosphate. Inverell, in fact, owes much of her commercial and financial importance to her mineral riches.

Twelve miles south of the Queensland border is the major New England centre of Tenterfield. The town is credited with being the birthplace of Australian Federation. It was in the local School of Arts on 24 October, 1889 that Sir Henry Parkes, then Premier of New South Wales, delivered a speech giving impetus to the movement which eventually brought about the creation of the Australian Commonwealth. The building has now been acquired by the National Trust, and serves as a public library. The section from which the speech was actually delivered is preserved as a Memorial Library, devoted to the display of historical records and relics associated with Sir Henry Parkes.

Tenterfield is the centre of a rich district noted primarily for its cattle, wool and fat lambs; but also producing maize, dairy products, honey, corn and cold-climate fruits. Tobacco, too, is grown, and it has one of the most important stock-trucking stations in the State.

Scenic attractions around the district include the Boonoo Boonoo Falls, prounced 'Bunna-Bernoo', where the stream falls 685 feet to the valley below. However, the access road to the falls is fairly rough, with numerous shallow streams crossing the winding road through bushland still in its natural state. Bald Rock is another natural feature not easy of access, yet worth the effort of reaching it. A rough, winding track leads to this mighty granite rock which is located in a flora and fauna sanctuary. Reminiscent of Ayers Rock, it overlooks views of deep valleys and blue-hazed hills.

Ghost Gully is especially popular with photographers seeking unusual effects in this heavily eroded area with strangely-shaped rocks protruding everywhere. An old Aboriginal corroboree ground may be seen at Boorook, where there are fossils and one of the many gossamer-spray waterfalls of the district.

Payable gold was found in the Tenterfield area for many years. One site was oddly-named 'Lunatic', which in its day had a population of several thousands. Then a prosperous mining town, it boasted no less than nineteen hotels. Its name perpetuates the prospector who discovered the original gold mine there, and who spent his last few shillings in buying tools to sink a shaft. He was nicknamed 'Lunatic' by those who knew him until he struck it rich. Soon many miners flocked to the scene and the township sprang up, named after its discoverer.

At a spot on willow-fringed Tenterfield Creek is Thunderbolt's Leap, so named from a daring exploit by the bushranger. He and Monkton, another outlaw, planned to raid the then bustling tin-mining centre of Emmaville. Surprised by two troopers after they had swum their horses across the flooded

Tenterfield Creek, the outlaws galloped into the dense bush with the troopers in hot pursuit until a wide, steep declivity blocked the way and it became a case of stand and fight, or leap for life. Both bushrangers spurred their horses into the gulf and escaped.

EIGHT

The Warrumbungles

On the southern edge of the New England plateau the volcanic Liverpool Range runs westward, culminating in the strange pinnacles and spires of the Warrumbungles in central New South Wales. Part of the Great Divide, the Liverpool Range is about 90 miles in length, flanked on the north by the Liverpool Plains and the upper tributaries of the Namoi River, and on the south by the Merriwa plateau and the headwaters of the Hunter-Goulburn system. The range is relatively narrow, with its peaks all about 3,700 feet high. Crossed near Murrurundi by the main northern railway and the New England highway, the range was named by explorer Oxley, after the second Earl of Liverpool, Prime Minister of Britain, in 1818.

Probably not more than one in ten thousand Australians has ever heard of the Warrumbungles; yet its 14,000 acres contain some of Australia's most spectacular mountain scenery, and groups of the world's rarest extinct volcanoes. Approaching from the western plains, one first sees the Warrumbungles as a low and jagged, almost grotesque, silhouette against the sky. Jutting abruptly from the plains, the ancient volcanic remnants look strangely out of place even in the mountain terrain of the Warrumbungle National Park. One finds elsewhere in Australia the great plugs of old volcanoes, or impressive extinct craters; but the Warrumbungles contain all of these and much more.

Both Needle Mountain and Siding Spring Mountain, where the Australian National University has established an observatory, are about 4,000 feet high. These peaks are on the perimeter of the park, and command magnificent views of the jagged crowns and steep valleys of the range, and of plains extending westwards into the distant haze.

One of the most fantastic formations in the Warrumbungles is 'The Breadknife', a sheer wall hundreds of feet high but only a few feet thick. Other remarkable formations are the Belougery Spire, Tonduron Spire, Crater Bluff, The Needle, and Bluff Mountain. The peaks are made still more attractive by their colouring. Where the early morning light falls directly, they are seen in their natural reddish colour; as shadows form, however, blue and red allternate, the blues becoming darker as more of the peak falls into shade, and passing through bluish purple to black as the setting sun leaves the massive pillars silhouetted against the sky.

When the Warrumbungles' volcanoes were active, the latter part of the lava flows was plastic rather than molten, and squeezed up from vents like tooth paste from a tube. When the volcanoes quietened, the plastic masses solidified. Millions of years, and wind and weather, eroded away most of the softer surrounding cones, leaving the solid plugs as vertical pillars towering into the air. The underlying sandstones of the Warrumbungles were laid down in a gigantic lake, filling the centre of Australia about 150 million years ago, in Jurassic times.

The park's two main walks are to the top of Mount Exmouth (4,025 feet), filling an energetic four hours; and a six-hour walk along the Pincham Trail. The latter has various short spur tracks leading to look-outs which reveal peaks, rugged gorges, and sharp precipices. Whether seen hard and clear-cut in the bright sunlight, or with the outlines of the peaks softened and diffused in blue haze, the scenery is dramatically beautiful.

Kangaroos and wallabies are plentiful, and there are many varieties of lizards; but snakes are rare. A friendly goanna may beg a crust or two, or steal one if possible. Let him be. Bird life is abundant: finches, butcher-birds, wagtails, and currawongs, to name a few, with, along the creeks, herons and brilliantly plumaged kingfishers. Some of the birds will perch on your rucksack and take food from your hands. Here, too, is seen the majestic Wedge-tailed eagle. Lord of the Australian skies, this soaring bird of prey with a wing span covering as much as three yards, builds an immense nest as wide as eight feet, and just as deep, high in an isolated tree-top. Many bird lovers regard the Wedge-tail as a finer bird than the renowned Golden eagle.

In spring the Warrumbungles become fragrant with the scent of flowering trees, native shrubs, and wildflowers: rosemary, flax lily, cassia, spider flower, boronia, flannel flower, waxlip orchid, pink fingers, lady's slipper and wild violets. Around here were the tribal grounds of the Kamilaroi Aborigines: Warrumbungle is their word, meaning a broken, or crooked mountain. Although they have long since disappeared, their tribal names live on in many towns of the surrounding country.

Canyon Camp is the headquarters of the park and the chief ranger's residence. Here, six old corridor trams, brought to the park on special timber jinkers, have been converted into visitor accommodation. Each has sleeping accommodation for four people, with a dining area and an all-electric kitchen. An amenities block is nearby. Of course, visitors can bring their own caravans and tents; several huts along the trails provide accommodation for the younger and more adventurous. Since the park is a complete sanctuary, the carrying of guns is prohibited. There is also a prohibition against climbing The Breadknife since stones could easily be dislodged and injure walkers on the path below it.

A spur range of the Great Divide branching from the New England plateau near the township of Kentucky is known as the Nandewar Range. A rickety backbone of brilliant blue mountains, the Nandewars, like the Warrumbungles, is of volcanic origin. West from the town of Barraba, it snakes its sinuous way northwards between Bingara and Narrabri, and finally disappears in the vicinity of Bellata.

Mount Kaputar, more than 5,000 feet in height, towers majestically above the rest of the range like a great clenched fist. This peak gives a panoramic view of rugged mountains (with the Warrumbungles in the dim distance), and of sprawling valleys extending into Queensland and the New

England Ranges. It is estimated that the view from Mount Kaputar takes in 30,000 square miles about a tenth of the whole of New South Wales.

Forming the watershed between the Namoi and Gwydir rivers, the many peaks and spires of the plateau are of incredible ruggedness, with a volcanic crater that overlooks gorges resembling giant knifecuts and others with sheer, castle-like walls. Apart from the mountains themselves, the Nandewars contain many places of unique and scientific interest including the Valley of the Devil's Holes, Castle Top and Yalladunida Crater. Temperatures in the Nandewars are very different from those on the plains below, being as much as 25 degrees lower, even in summer. Snow is no novelty in winter; and at times the whole range is white above the 3,500 feet line.

A newly-constructed road links the Nandewars with the town of Narrabri: and at nearby Dawson Springs caravan and camping facilities, as well as cabins, are available for visitors.

NINE

Remarkable Women

AT the foot of the Moonbi Range, in the rich Peel River Valley, lies the solid and prosperous city of Tamworth, the first country centre in Australia to have its streets lit at night by electricity. That was in 1888; and Tamworth commemorates the fact with its annual Festival of Light. The city's population of 21,000 or more has an excellent art gallery and public library, fine public buildings, and churches, enhanced by well-kept parks and gardens. There are several important schools, including the Farrer Memorial Agricultural High School.

The railway from Newcastle to Tamworth was completed in 1878, but connection with Sydney was not made until ten years later, with the completion of the first Hawkesbury River bridge. Traversing the district is a wide metalliferous belt, carrying tin, copper and other metals; and there is also a large area of limestone deposits. Overlooking Tamworth, and about 800 feet above it, is Oxley Park, 1,000 acres in area. Both the Peel River and Tamworth itself are named to commemorate Sir Robert Peel, who represented the Staffordshire town of Tamworth in the British Parliament.

The Moonbi Lookout, at the top of the first steep pass of the Moonbi Range, is on the crest of a great granite boulder with steps cut into the rock face. With Hanging Rock, atop a mountain reached by a precipitous winding road, in and among mountain scenery of rare grandeur, this is among the attractions of the district.

Southward, the Great Divide includes the Mount Royal

Range, with a wide-spread plateau known as Barrington Tops. The plateau is the source of several rivers, including the Manning, Barrington, Gloucester and Paterson. With an altitude ranging to some 5,200 feet, the plateau is threaded by trails, and is admirable for bushwalking or horse-riding; while its many streams lure the trout fisherman. Part of the plateau— the Barrington Brush—is remarkable for its growth of unique specimens of wild-flowers, and the dense underbrush at the foot of snow gums and giant antarctic beeches.

Barrington Tops and the Mount Royal Range form part of the inland area of the rich Hunter Valley region, where inland and on the coast lie the huge coal-seams that were once the basis of Sydney's and Newcastle's power resources, and which still make an important contribution to them. Just about every branch of rural activity is encompassed within the 10,000 square miles of this fertile valley, the oldest commercial grape-growing area in Australia, where the first wine grapes were grown in the 1830s.

In its early history this was the domain of the fabulous Molly Morgan, the rat-catcher's daughter, who died a wealthy woman with the local title of 'Queen of the Hunter Valley'. Much of the site of the city of Maitland was then known as 'Molly Morgan's Plains'.

Born in Shropshire, Molly Jones was a pert, rosy-cheeked, wanton baggage when she married William Morgan, a wheelwright and carpenter, to whom she bore two children. She was already the mother of a child whose father, a well-to-do farmer, refused to marry her. To provide a little extra for the struggling family, Molly succumbed to the temptation of stealing a few yards of hempen yarn. Her pilfering was detected and she was brought to trial, and sentenced to transportation for five years. She was lucky, the bewigged and scarlet-robed judge told her solemnly. If the stolen goods had been worth a few more shillings she would have hanged by her pretty white neck from the gallows outside Shrewsbury prison.

Although she sailed for Botany Bay aboard the hell-ship, *Neptune*—one of the vessels of the second fleet—Molly Morgan's good looks and easy virtue gained her many privileges, and she endured little of the sufferings of other convicts. When the

Neptune, Surprise, and *Scarborough* left England they had nearly 1,000 male and female felons crowded between their stinking, verminous decks. By the time they reached Sydney, nearly 300 had died from sickness and ill-treatment and most of the survivors were skeletons of diseased skin and bone, shaking with fever and scarcely able to crawl.

But there were some who tripped ashore blithely enough. During the long voyage there had never been any shortage of rations or comforts for handsome and willing convict girls like Molly Morgan. Even on arrival in Sydney, the merry-eyed Molly saw her prison guards vying for her favours. It was not long before she was transferred to Parramatta where she was practically a free agent—a move that suited her very well indeed.

Life was hard and lonely for the military guards and over-seers. Molly generously did her best to provide them with the comforts of home, and in return no one expected her to toil with the other bedraggled convict hussies. Set up in a neat cottage, she tended a small farm and peddled grog, which she cajoled out of her soldier admirers.

Three years after her arrival in the colony, her husband, William Morgan, came with a new batch of prisoners also transported for stealing. Because of his good behaviour, William was allowed to live with Molly; but he soon raised objections to his wife's scandalous conduct with soldier friends. This was a handicap to the saucy wench, and she decided to escape from the environment. She listened avidly to stories of convicts who had made their escape in ships calling at Sydney Cove, usually with the connivance of whaling skippers or traders.

Early in 1794 her chance came when, on a trip to Sydney Town, she met Captain Locke of the whaler *Resolution*. While in a grog den on the waterfront, she asked the half-tipsy captain if he would take her back to England, in return for her favours. The proposition was accepted and, indeed, the skipper found her so pleasing on the long voyage that, when his vessel arrived in England, he offered her a permanent home on the *Resolution* as his companion. She declined and, after collecting her children from relatives who were looking after them, moved to Plymouth where she worked as a seamstress.

A prosperous brassfounder, Thomas Mares, proposed marriage to Molly, and although she had a husband working out his sentence in far-off Australia, she accepted. The 'marriage' was happy enough in its early stages, but following a quarrel 'Mad Molly' (as her friends called her) set fire to Mares' home, and it was burned to the ground. Infuriated, Mares called in the police; but the fire-bug had escaped to London. There she was caught and at the Croydon Quarter Sessions on 10 October, 1803, was sentenced for the second time to transportation.

Fortunately for this lucky prisoner she still had good looks and a much admired figure, so it is not surprising that in a short time she was the holder of a ticket-of-leave. She was fortunate, too, inasmuch as her rightful husband, William Morgan, bothered her not at all on his release, but quietly disappeared from the scene. Molly, with the help of a 'protector', a member of the Parramatta garrison, acquired a few acres of land and some horses and cattle.

Prosperity came quickly. Her herds increased so rapidly that, when puzzled officials investigated, they found that many of the beasts were ones reported as stolen. Her freedom lost, the incorrigible Molly was sent to the Coal River convict camp. Once again her charms came to her rescue and, although now in her forty-fourth year, she dazzled the military men in this womanless penal outpost, and they treated her more like a guest than a prisoner. So another ticket-of-leave was soon forthcoming.

Molly was more than ever determined to amass riches, and to do so quickly; but in a more or less legitimate enterprise. She decided, too, to remain in the Hunter River district where she had so many men friends and admirers. Cedar-getters and settlers were moving into the fertile valley, and Molly Morgan opened a rough grog shanty for the thirsty newcomers, as well as the troops, and coal miners in the newly discovered coal-fields. The slab and bark shanty was well patronised, and in about 1818, Molly opened an inn at Wallis Plains, on the present site of Maitland. Her hostelry—the Angel Inn—stood opposite where the post-office now stands, and proved a magnet for the increasing population of the prosperous district.

The buxom, bold-eyed proprietress was the toast of the town. She amassed riches enough to be considered one of the wealthiest in the colony, and certainly the richest in the district where she lived. At Wallis Plains, much better known as Molly Morgan's Plains, she bought up large blocks of river-frontage land, and all the area that now comprises the main business centre of West Maitland.

Governor Brisbane so admired her success that he gave her the use of convict gangs to clear her land. Despite the fact that she was still legally married, she went through another 'marriage ceremony' with Thomas Hunt, a handsome young garrison soldier. Yet even in her sixties she remained sprightly and shapely, and always a shrewd and clever businesswoman. On one occasion she made a wild non-stop ride to Sydney in a last-minute attempt to plead with the Governor to spare the lives of some convicts sentenced to be executed for stealing fruit from an orchard. Her intercession saved them from the gallows. Little wonder that Molly Morgan was revered as the 'Queen of the Hunter Valley'. Before her death in 1833, she had subdivided her land and sold it in small blocks for business premises and residential sites, and had retired to her 200-acre farm at Anvil Creek, near Greta.

The Manning, a coastal stream which rises not far from Barrington Tops in the Mount Royal Range, is only about 140 miles in length, but it is fed by many important tributaries which drain a considerable area of the eastern highlands and the Mount Royal Range. The upper reaches of the Manning and its tributaries are heavily timbered, and are a source of much high-grade eucalypt hardwood. The lower Manning runs through rich agricultural and dairying country which produces milk, butter, maize and vegetables. The chief towns of the flourishing valley are Taree, Wingham, and Gloucester.

In the Manning River country, during the middle of the last century, there lived another extraordinary pioneer, Isabella Mary Kelly, a woman who ruled the district with a rod of iron. Few records of her remain; but it is known that she was a sadistic flogger of convicts and a ruthless killer of the Aborigines. Even darker deeds have been hinted at.

The rugged country of the Nandewars, New South Wales   (page 66)

*Ghost Gully, near Tenterfield, is popular with photographers
seeking unusual effects*   (page 62)

Why Isabella Kelly chose to lose herself in the wilds of a newly-settled outpost will never be known. Along the Manning River, old-timers still tell strange stories of this mysterious woman; legends handed down the years, and probably embroidered in the process; but undoubtedly true in the main. They are all of them grim.

Isabella Kelly came from Ireland, of a well-to-do family, and had received a good education. According to reports, she was engaged to be married to an army officer in Dublin. It was to be a big social wedding, and elaborate preparations were made for it; but on the wedding-day the bridegroom failed to arrive at the church. Her jilted romance so embittered her that she fled from her friends and surroundings, and came to Australia.

All the stories told on the Manning River agree on her imperious temper, belligerence and overbearing character. She was about twenty-five years old when she arrived in the district, with some thirty assigned convict servants. Nobody is sure when she first took up the Brimbin and Mount George properties in the Taree district, but she used them both for raising cattle and horses. Whether she had any authority to squat on the very large area embraced by the two properties is doubtful; but she was definitely in occupation in 1832, and practically the only settler between Stroud and Port Macquarie.

By the following year she was well established and had about 300 head of stock. She ran her properties single-handed, meting out punishment to the convicts in a manner better imagined than described. The law stated that when convicts needed punishment they were to be dealt with by the public scourger. But Isabella Kelly defied authority, and flogged the convicts herself.

When a tribe of Aborigines killed a few head of her cattle she went to Dungog, where she demanded that the police magistrate, Captain Thomas Cook, send out an armed expedition to deal with the natives. Cook refused; and Miss Kelly violently abused him, vowing that she would attend to the matter herself. Returning home, she armed herself with a rifle and pistol, and slaughtered the small Aboriginal population. Even that did not stir the Chief Secretary, and this infamous woman continued her reign of terror.

One day, towards the end of 1840, she set off with a consignment of hides and tallow to be sold at Maitland. Two convicts were in charge of the load, and she accompanied them on horseback. On the return trip, as they were crossing the range at Wallarobba, they were bailed up by a gang of bushrangers led by Edward Davis—known as the Jewboy. The gang didn't bother the two convicts, but they tied Isabella to a wheel of the dray, took a pistol from her, and stole the £60 she had been paid for the hides and tallow.

When the gang left, she ordered the convicts to set her free. She had another pistol concealed in her saddle-bag, and she set off after the bushrangers. She caught up with them after a five-mile chase and opened fire, one bullet striking a bushranger in the shoulder. She made them give up not only her own money, but other money they had in their possession. Eventually the members of this gang were rounded up by the troopers and hanged in Sydney.

On another occasion she decided to take two of her convicts to Port Macquarie and have them put in the solitary confinement cells in the penal settlement there. Saddling up her horse, and with her pistols round her belt, she marched off. On the way they were crossing a flooded river when her horse was swept from under her and she was thrown into the swiftly-flowing waters. One of the convicts, risking his own life, swam out after her and saved her from drowning. She showed her gratitude by forcing her saviour and his companion to continue marching to the penal settlement, where she had them thrown into the dungeons.

By the 1860s Isabella Kelly was a wealthy woman; her properties had greatly prospered. But now there was considerable settlement on the Manning, and newcomers began to squat on portions of the big territory which Miss Kelly claimed was her land. Finding that she could not scare them away, and unwilling to risk the drastic personal action that succeeded in the past when settlers were few (during the 1840s she fired at and wounded a newcomer who had the temerity to squat on a small portion of her land), she invoked the law. That settled her.

The Government appointed a Select Committee to inquire into her title. It was then found that she had no proof that any land grants had been made to her. Furthermore, she had taken no steps to record her title to any of the land.

The reign of Isabella Kelly, the woman who had ruled and terrorized the district for nearly thirty years, was over. She moved to Sydney, and soon afterwards sailed for England. However, she returned later to end her days in Sydney; she died in 1897, friendless, alone, and almost forgotten. It is said she compiled her life story for publication, but the manuscript disappeared after her death. It would have been a valuable historic document of the pioneering days, but it is doubtful if Isabella Kelly would have recorded the whole of her life story—there were so many sinister episodes.

TEN

The Burning Mountain

THE Hunter valley is bounded on all sides by ranges or hills, though in the west, particularly near Cassilis, the Great Dividing Range is only gently sloping. It has been estimated that about three-fifths of the land in the valley slopes too steeply for use: in the upper parts flat land is restricted to the floors of the various river valleys, and only east of about Singleton does the Hunter emerge into wide plains. On the undulating and hilly country of the valley sheep-raising and cattle-raising are the principal activities, while on the rich river flats dairying is a most important industry.

The big northern coalfield of New South Wales falls within the valley area; Newcastle, Maitland, Cessnock, Greta, and Muswellbrook being among the mining areas. Manufacturing is centred on Newcastle, with its great iron and steel works and related industries; manufactures in other areas include rayon textiles, milk products, and building boards.

Probably the first white people to reach the Hunter, and to find coal there, were a party of escaped convicts led by William Bryant in 1791. Five years later a fishing party brought back to Sydney several pieces of coal that were probably obtained from near Newcastle. In 1797 Lieutenant John Shortland discovered a 'fine coal river' to which he gave Governor Hunter's name. (The name Coal River was, however, in use for a number of years.) The rich coal seam which Shortland discovered may still be seen today in the cliffside.

Though 1797 is taken as Newcastle's foundation date, the

city's 150th anniversary celebrations being held in 1947, a settlement was not actually established there until 1801. Three years later Governor King named the town Newcastle and the surrounding district Northumberland, after the city of Newcastle and county of Northumberland in England. One of the most important single events in the history of Newcastle and surrounding districts was the establishment in 1825 of the Australian Agricultural Company. This organization, which played a big part in developing the district during the nineteenth century, is still a going concern. While it was primarily interested in the growth of pastoral resources, the company's main significance in relation to Newcastle was its development of the coalfields. Coal enticed people and industry to Newcastle; ships came from almost every port in the world, until Newcastle harbour became a regular forest of masts and sails. Symbolic of the development of the period is the fact that the foreshores of Stockton are built on the ballast of craft unloaded there for more than fifty years.

Newcastle is undoubtedly a city of enterprise, with a massive industrial, commercial and transportation complex. Great expansion is still taking place in the city and its environs. The second city of New South Wales and the sixth-largest in Australia (it is bigger than Canberra and Hobart), Newcastle is one of the most important centres in the Commonwealth for the manufacture of steel and steel products. Besides the gigantic Broken Hill Proprietary steelworks, it is the site of the New South Wales State Dockyard and is the headquarters of many other important industrial undertakings. The B.H.P. steelworks has more than 11,500 employees, with its own fire and medical services, its own guards, its own ships and railway system.

Understandably, because of its power resources, the Hunter Valley region is the site of several huge power-stations, in full or part operation, or still under construction. By 1970 the region will produce 80 per cent of the power requirements of New South Wales. While lavish enough with its gifts, the Hunter Valley has struck back savagely at times, when man has disturbed the balance of nature too greatly in his exploitation of the riches of the region. Since 1900 the valley has suffered some thirty major floods and droughts; but the researches of governmental and other authorities are gradually overcoming the danger of floods and the hazards of dry seasons.

Inland may be seen one of the most interesting of Australia's natural wonders—Mount Wingen, better known as the 'Burning Mountain'. This is a ridge rising about 800 feet directly from the valley of the Page River, a tributary of the Hunter. From fissures in the hillside are emitted volumes of smoke produced by the combustion of a thick coal-seam, and also the vapours of sulphur compounds which coat the heated rock-surfaces in the vicinity with a lemon-yellow deposit.

Wingen, named from an Aboriginal word meaning 'fire', lies midway between Murrurundi and Scone. Scientists believe that the fire probably started some thousands of years ago, perhaps from heat generated by the oxidation of sulphur in pyrites, or maybe through a burning tree falling across the coal output. The slow combustion is due to the scanty supply of oxygen underneath.

As in other countries of the world, coal-strikes have resulted in the loss to Australia of thousands of tons of coal; but all such man-caused losses are infinitesimal compared with the coal wastage at Mount Wingen. It is strange to think that the hissing and rumbling coal fires here were burning before the first known navigators touched Australia's shores; before Columbus sighted America; thousands of years before Christianity, even. It can be seen from the New England Highway or, as it is on private property, may be inspected by appointment. There is no road to it from the highway, but a walk of less than two miles is comparatively easy. About two miles north of the village of Wingen, one leaves the highway near the overhead bridge, and walks in a south-easterly direction.

The first published reference to Mount Wingen appeared in the bi-weekly journal, the *Australian*, in March 1828. The news caused quite a sensation in Sydney Town.

'A volcano', exulted the *Australian*, 'has just been discovered in the vicinity of the Hunter River . . . in a north-westerly direction from Newcastle—12 miles beyond Holdsworthy Plains, and 14 miles from Segenhoe.

'Of the existence of the phenomenon there can be no doubt. It has been visited by several persons. When discovered the volcano emitted a brilliant light.'

The writer added: 'The composition which rolls from the surface readily ignites, and, without any test besides burning, the sulphuric smell which accompanies the flame immediately betokens its nature.'

The report came from information given by one of a party of the earlier settlers of the upper Hunter, who, when hunting in the ranges above the present town of Scone, saw smoke issuing from a hillside to the east. Aborigines accompanying the party had said that the smoke came from a burning mountain, which they called Wingen.

To investigate this supposed new Stromboli, an expedition was sent from Sydney. The party was keenly interested in scientific matters, but with evidently more enthusiasm for than deep knowledge of volcanoes. On their return, the investigators prepared a fulsome report, which was published in the *Australian*. It aroused such interest that the Reverend Charles P. N. Wilton, an experienced geologist, set out in the following year to see for himself the 'volcano' of which all Sydney was talking. He soon debunked the expedition's report. Writing to the *Sydney Gazette*, Wilton said: 'The description of this mountain is entirely incorrect, for in the first place there is *no* mouth or crater at all. No doubt the clefts in the mountain caused the party to give them the appellation of crater. The fact is, the rock, as the subterraneous fire increases, is rent into several concave chasms of various widths.'

In 1906, Professor Edgeworth David, Professor of Geology, stated that the seam of coal providing fuel for the subterranean fire was burning something like 1,500 feet below the surface of Mount Wingen. His theory that the fire was caused by spontaneous combustion now has general support.

Nearly two miles north from the present position of the fire is the Little Burning Mountain; and it was on this mountain that Mr C. J. Ivin, a qualified geologist, located the fossil leaves of a plant previously unknown to paleo-botany. It has been named *Annularia ivini*, in recognition of his discovery.

On the side of Burning Mountain itself fossils are common. Two fossils, bearing some resemblance to the common mussel of the western rivers, and a scalloped fan-shaped shell, found so abundantly on the east coast beaches, are easily enough recovered fairly close to the fire.

Close observation was kept on the fire between 1862 and 1924 by Mr W. E. Abbott, whose observations are among the best available. He reported that during the last sixty-five years there had been a gradual lessening of the fire as it moved south, but in 1917, 'it flared up, and is now sending out greater volumes of smoke than it did in the recollection of the writer'. Mr Abbott's findings are recorded in a small book, printed only for private circulation, unfortunately, and now difficult to come by. It mentions that the fire moved (burning continuously) no more than a yard a year, so that at the time of the book's publication it had not moved more than about sixty-five yards in sixty-five years.

In the 1930s, Burning Mountain was sending out great volumes of smoke and sulphurous fumes. Although at present the fire is greatly subdued, it is still burning fiercely on a 'face' about a chain wide, and there are many vents and crevices a few feet deep from which comes smoke, and very considerable heat. The earth will not bear handling; pure yellow sulphur is on the side of the vents; and the stones are white from the great heat.

Visitors are invariably puzzled as to why the weight of earth and rocks pressing down upon the fire, now estimated to be about five hundred feet from the surface, has not crushed it. The reason is that the coal seam and surrounding rocks both 'dip' steeply to the west. Evidence of this can be seen in the crevices on the western side. As the coal is consumed by the fire, the rocks above, being inclined, keep the great weight of earth from falling upon the fire. This formation, in addition to keeping the weight of stone and earth from crushing the fire, has also allowed just sufficient oxygen to keep it consuming a few feet of the coal seam each year.

Some authorities estimate that the fire has travelled underground at the rate of about 123 yards per century. Nevertheless, to the geologists, thinking in terms of thousands of years, the end of the burning mountain is in sight. Many generations will probably pass before the fire reaches the summit of Mount Wingen, but when it does, its eventual extinction will not be so very far distant. In the meantime, it remains one of the many unique natural wonders of Australia.

ELEVEN

The Road Builders

SOUTHWARD of the Liverpool Range is the Hunter Range, which lies generally to the west of Maitland. The term 'Blue Mountains' is sometimes applied loosely to the highlands between the Hunter Range in the north and the vicinity of the city of Goulburn in the south; geologically there is some justification for its use. More accurately, the Blue Mountains are an eastern spur of the Great Dividing Range, lying between the lower Nepean and upper Hawkesbury rivers on the east, and the Cox River on the west.

The mountains were first sighted by Governor Phillip when he was exploring the northern shore of Port Jackson in April 1788. He originally gave the name, 'Carmarthen Hills' to the northern part of the highlands, and called the southern part the 'Landsdowne Hills'; but within a few years the term Blue Mountains was in common use, owing to the vivid hue they take on when viewed from a distance. Shortly after Governor Macquarie arrived in Sydney town in December 1809, he found that the colony had been much neglected; there was no revenue, and famine had plagued the colony for years. He was very keen to have the country further explored, as the main settlement was hemmed in by the Blue Mountains, and it was thought that there must be a great territory beyond. In the year 1813 there was a severe drought which carried off many cattle and sheep, while the scarcity of grass threatened to ruin the settlers. This induced a further attempt to cross the Blue Mountains.

For upwards of twenty-five years after the founding of the settlement in the year 1788, on the shores of Sydney Cove, that great natural barrier, the Blue Mountains, successfully defied every effort made to scale their formidable heights and penetrate into the unknown country beyond. Times out of number, expeditions were despatched from Sydney with this object in view, only to return, after weeks of toil and hardship, baffled and dispirited. Again and again, such names as George Bass, Ensign Barrallier, William Caley, Henry Hacking, and even Governor Macquarie himself, set out with high hopes of overcoming this obstacle to progress and spread of settlement; only to acknowledge themselves beaten in the end.

So matters went on until the autumn of the year 1813 when Gregory Blaxland (who had already made one or two attempts to solve the problem) hit upon a new plan of procedure, and, hastily consulting with William Charles Wentworth, and Lieutenant William Lawson of the Royal Victoria Company, whom he asked to join him in the expedition, started out from his farm at South Creek with four assistants and some horses, and on the evening of the same day camped at the foot of the first range.

On several days they were obliged to hew a passage for themselves and the horses through the dense brushwood, so that progress was slow and painful; many times it was found necessary to mark out the track to be followed on the succeeding day, return to camp, and in the morning proceed to form a path along the marked line, coming back to their camp again in the evening. They had thus to traverse their track several times, going and returning from work; and this added greatly to their fatigue. The scarcity of water was an ever-present trouble, and on one occasion it was necessary to descend a precipice about six hundred feet in depth in order to procure supplies for the camp.

On about the twelfth day, they reached the edge of what is now called the King's Tableland, and gazed with wonder into the great depths below them. It is this stage of their journey which moved Henry Kendall to write in his poem, the *Mountain Pioneers*, the lines:

'They fought with Nature till they reached the throne
Where morning glittered on the great unknown.'

On the eighteenth day out, the date being 28 May, they finally emerged on the ridge which terminates in the spur now known as Mount York. Here they camped for a day, after leading the horses down the almost perpendicular sides of the mountains in quest of water, and returning again to their camp at the summit. On the following day they were successful in discovering an easier passage to the valley below, between two great masses of rocks, where the first road was made, later on.

They now proceeded over a fine stretch of country, well-watered, and with abundance of grass. About eight miles further on, they reached the foot of a conical hill which later on received the name of Mount Blaxland, in honour of the explorer. From the summit of this eminence, they saw with delight the fertile country to the westward—their task had been accomplished. Losing little time, they began the return journey, eager to bring the news of their discovery to those who awaited the result. Their provisions were nearly expended, their clothes and boots were in a deplorable condition, and the whole party were more or less suffering from various ailments brought on by exposure and insufficient food. Nevertheless, the return journey was made in good time, and the Sydney settlement rejoiced to hear of the good country beyond the Blue Mountains.

Even the members of the expedition, however, little realized the tremendous possibilities of the newly discovered land which, in the coming years, would be fully utilized. They were the forerunners, too, of a band of explorers who eventually were destined to push their outposts farther and still farther west until, before the lapse of half a century, the limits of New South Wales had been pushed out for thousands of miles north, south and west.

In 1813, acting under instructions from Governor Macquarie, Deputy-Surveyor George William Evans explored the newly-discovered western district, starting from Blaxland's terminal point. Two years later he was sent on a second expedition, and welcomed Governor Macquarie and party on their arrival at the future site of the city of Bathurst in the same year. In a Government order dated 12 February, 1814, full particulars are given of Evans' expedition; and his remarkable diary, wherein each day's progress is set down, is one of the most interesting documents preserved in Australia.

The party started in November, five months after Blaxland's return with the news of his discovery. It consisted of five men, selected for their general knowledge of the country, and 'habituated to such difficulties as might be expected to occur.' Evans was well-supplied with horses, arms and ammunition, and a plentiful supply of provisions for a two months' trek. Five days after leaving the Nepean River, the party arrived at the terminal point of Blaxland's expedition, and then continued in a westerly direction for twenty-one days before making the return journey. During his trip Evans passed over several plains of great extent, abounding in the richest soil, and with various streams of water and chains of ponds. These plains were interspersed with hills and valleys.

The greater part of the plains was described by Evans as being nearly free of timber or brushwood, and in capacity equal, in his opinion, 'to every demand that the colony may make for an extension of tillage and pasture lands for a century to come'. How these words must have heartened the despairing settlers, whose experience of drought and famine had been of such a bitter nature, prior to Blaxland's discovery. From the crest of some high hills, Evans beheld a vast extent of magnificent country, lying in a westerly direction, which he named Bathurst Plains; and on part of this area, the city of Bathurst was eventually laid out.

The general description given by Evans of these hitherto unexplored regions, upon which the eyes of white men had never before rested, was that they 'surpassed in beauty and fertility of soil any that he had seen in the colonies'. As the first white man to complete the entire passage of the Blue Mountains, George Evans has attained a celebrity which will always entitle him to a high place among the worthy army of pioneers who have done so much for the country of their adoption.

A practical passage across the mountains having now been found, the next and most urgent question was the formation of a road to the newly discovered country, so that immediate use of the thousands of acres of rich land could be made. The likeliest man in the colony to make the road and superintend its construction was William Cox of Clarendon, the chief magistrate. He had a name for fair dealing, for stern integrity, and for capacity in dealing with men.

To Blaxland, Wentworth, and Lawson belongs the honour of first discovering a way over the Blue Mountains, and blazing the track for Evans to follow in their footsteps; but William Cox is deserving of equal credit for his remarkable engineering feat of building a road across these rugged heights, and thereby rendering the newly discovered territory available to the settlers. That extraordinary road, begun in July 1814, was finished in a little more than six months. It is almost unbelievable that such a mighty task could have been accomplished, under such conditions, in such a comparatively short space of time. The road commenced at Emu Ford, on the left bank of the Nepean River, and finished at the flagstaff at Bathurst, covering a distance of 102 miles.

Cox's caravan, and horse and bullock carts were the first wheeled vehicles to pass over the Blue Mountains and down over Mount York, on 5 December, 1814. When Cox's road was completed, Governor and Mrs Macquarie, with a Vice-Regal party, and servants, set out to visit the newly discovered country west of the Blue Mountains. On reaching Mount York, the Governor named that part of the road Cox's Pass. They continued as far as Glenroy, and here, on Sunday, 30 April, the first divine service west of the Blue Mountains was held. The following Sunday, Governor Macquarie christened the intended town of Bathurst, and again held divine service.

The grade of Cox's Pass, down Mount York to the Vale of Clwydd, was one in four; the descent was so steep that huge logs or trunks of trees had to be attached to the rear of a vehicle to act as a drag, so as to prevent it from running away and being smashed to pieces. Governor Macquarie wrote in his journal that on 29 April, 1815, his party reached the termination of the Blue Mountains, ending in a very abrupt descent—almost perpendicular. 'Here we halted for a little while to view this frightful, tremendous pass, as well as to feast our eyes with the grand and pleasing prospect of the fine low country below us.'

Writing to a friend in England in 1822, a Mrs Hawkins, who had just arrived from England, tells of setting out with her husband and family to make a new home on the recently opened plains beyond the Blue Mountains. She says: 'We had a waggon with six bullocks, a dray with five, another with three horses, a cart with two, and last of all, a tilted cart with my mother, myself, and seven children with two horses, while Mr Hawkins and a son were mounted.' She mentions the continual terror they experienced when the road led them past such precipices 'as would make you shudder'. On the day they descended Mount York, and had to chain trees behind the drays, 'the tree that we chained behind the last dray was 48 feet long, and at the extremity, on the bough were seated three men.'

What of the builders of the road? Between the townships of Woodford and Linden is the site of Captain Bull's Camp, which was occupied in the 1830s by a large party of the military and convicts, the latter engaged in the construction of the then new road. Nearby in the scrub are the graves of several soldiers belonging to the Eightieth Regiment who had died whilst on duty, and were buried in the vicinity of the camp. To the west of the camp is still to be seen a flat space of rock, deeply scored with parallel grooves about six inches apart. This was known as the flogging stone. The grooves were for the purpose of preventing the executioner's feet from slipping when using his deadly instrument of torture. A 'dark cell' excavated in the rocks a few feet away is also another silent witness to the methods of the 'system' in vogue in those dark days.

It seems that the first stockade erected in New South Wales for road gangs working in irons for punishment was located in the narrow valley between Mounts York and Victoria, and the next was under Mount Walker, twelve miles west—a larger stockade than the other, and housing from 700 to 800 prisoners. The surveyor William Govett, after whom Govett's Leap at Blackheath is named, wrote: 'The prisoners are guarded by day and night. They march out of the stockade in the morning in companies of twenty-four each, guarded by two soldiers and a constable. Every man receives at the gates the tools he uses at work; shovels, picks, iron bars, and hatchets, all to be returned to the proper person when they return to the stockade at night.' The stockade consisted of rows of wooden huts in the form of a square, enclosed by a strong, fifteen foot high barrier with two big gates. Facing the gates outside the stockade were the soldiers' barracks. All the buildings were of slabs, with bark roofs, except the officers' quarters which were shingled. If a prisoner escaped, the soldier responsible would be court-martialled. A pound of fresh beef and a pound of bread represented the daily diet, with soup every other day.

When walking up the Victoria Pass between the great frowning masses of rock which have been literally carved out by brute strength, one sees that every inch of it is solid iron- and sand-stone, hard enough to turn the edge of the stoutest tool. A whole mountain has been removed bodily, and the resultant debris thrown into the valley to form the foundation of the giant causeway which carries the roadway to the further side. To preserve the road, and prevent the embankments so formed from sliding away, huge stone buttresses seventy or eighty feet in height have been formed with great blocks of cut and dressed stone. These are surmounted by a balustrade, with dwarf pillars every few feet.

On a portion of the rock cutting near the upper end of the Pass there is a sinister inscription, cut by unskilled hands, but plainly visible to this day. Only two words appear on the rock: 'Connelly Escaped'. It is a record of the daring and successful escape of one of the road gang, who managed to dodge about a dozen bullets and got clean away; what became of him eventually has never been ascertained. The man was a notorious character, and at the time of the escape was working in double irons, being also closely marked by the sentries. He watched his opportunity, however, and though heavily handicapped by his manacles, made a sudden dash, and was out of sight in a moment. His mates, overcome with pride at the daring of the man, decided to record the feat in the imperishable rock; and so the inscription remains, a curious confirmation of history.

There are about twelve kinds of ringtailed possums. All are
arboreal (page 37)

'Cascades rush in splashing ribbons of silver.' Katoomba Falls, Blue Mountains   (page 89)

TWELVE

The Blue Mountains

THE Blue Mountains area extends for eighty miles from Lapstone to Mount Victoria atop the Great Dividing Range. It encompasses twenty-four separate townships, with an area of 550 square miles; the majority of the townships straddling the Great Western Highway, which leads to the fertile western districts of the State. Easily and comfortably reached by road or rail from Sydney in a few hours, the Blue Mountains provide popular day trips for visitors whose time is limited.

Nature required several hundred thousand years to mould these mountains into a masterpiece of scenic beauty. Their geological structure renders what is seen there phenomenal; often awesome, or startlingly grand. Streams do not trickle off the central hump-backed ridge—they plunge, spray-veiled, sheer over thousand-foot cliffs. Down in the glens and gorges, cascades rush in splashing ribbons of silver through mighty stands of timber, natural boulder-strewn amphitheatres here and there patched pale green with carpets of moss; grottos choked with ferns, where bird-calls mingle with the music of swirling water.

From look-outs and other vantage points along the central ridge can be seen broad valleys hemmed in by stark, perpendicular cliffs. Distant roofs of valley forests present ever-changing patchworks of colour—green, mauve, blue, purple. Towering in solitude from valley floors far below, giant masses of sandstone stand like grotesque sentinels in pink, grey and pale gold,

some bearing absurd headdresses of scrub. Many such panoramic views—sweeping landscapes of nature at her grandest and
loveliest—are unique to the Blue Mountains: the blue haze, the
verdure, the waterfalls, the coloured rock formations, give the
Blue Mountains a living vividness with which no other place in
Australia can be compared.

The Katoomba, Leura and Blackheath areas exhibit some of
the strangest and most spectacular mountain scenery in the
entire region. And no other route reveals so much of it within
so short a distance as the famous five-mile Cliff Drive. First the
vast Megalong Valley is seen intermittently through breaks in
roadside clumps of trees; and then, Cahill's Look-out. Where
the Drive emerges at Narrow Neck Plateau, both the Megalong
and Jamieson Valleys suddenly appear in all their glory—
immense blue, mauve and purple depressions, irregularly
walled in by sheer cliffs, rust and pink coloured. Half a mile
further on, the Drive reaches its apex at Cyclorama Lookout,
the highest point in Katoomba; and here a delicately tinted
panorama takes in the Megalong and Jamieson Valleys, the
steep cliffs of Narrow Neck, the Ruined Castle, Saddleback and
Mount Solitary. When visibility is good, Mount Jellore at
Mittagong can be seen in one direction, and the sands of
Botany Bay in the opposite—each more than sixty miles away.
The scenery is astonishing and spell-binding, all the way to the
Drive's terminus at Gordon Falls; it includes the Katoomba
Falls, Malaita Point, Eagle Hawk Rock, The Three Sisters,
Echo Point and Leura Falls.

Blackheath, about seven miles along the Great Western
Highway from Katoomba, features scenery spectacular enough
to have astonished Charles Darwin. Viewing Blackheath Gorge,
the great scientist described it as the largest chasm on earth
with perpendicular sides. Nearby is the impressive Govett's
Leap, and the Bridal Veil Falls, a milk-white column of water
that plunges 1,000 feet from plateau to valley floor. Every
year, in November, Blackheath stages a Rhododendron
Festival, when more than a thousand varieties of the genus
bursts into profuse and incredibly colourful bloom. These
flowering shrubs, the most prolific of their kind in the Common-

wealth, have won prizes from some of the world's leading gardeners and horticulturists.

'Everglades', a glorious twelve-and-a-half acre property, is open for inspection. Natural bushland, exotic trees and flowers, meet and blend in perfect harmony; and the gardens and grottos are justifiably renowned. In 1962 the property was acquired by the National Trust of Australia which has restored and established it as the first Australian national garden and cold-climate arboretum.

For bush hikers, the Grand Canyon and Rodriguez Pass at Blackheath, the National Pass Walk at Wentworth Falls, the Minnehaha Falls, Prince Henry Cliff and Federal Pass Walks at Katoomba provide unusual bush trails of sheer delight. The Federal Pass Walk, for instance, about four miles in length and requiring about two and a half hours, skirts the foot of the cliffs between Leura and Katoomba Falls. The descent is made near Leura Falls by way of over thirteen hundred well-graded steps that wind down through corridors of mountain ash, cedar, bloodwoods and ghost gums, and through arcades of black-stumped tree-ferns; and tunnel, here and there, beneath tangles of lush flowering vines. Before reaching its end at the foot of the Katoomba Falls (where ascent may be made by the Scenic Railway), the track passes several waterfalls and cascades and the conspicuous Three Sisters.

The Scenic Railway, reputed to be the steepest in the world, drops 750 feet into the Jamieson Valley on a track 1,360 feet in length—a fall of more than one in two. The Scenic Skyway takes passengers from one cliff to another in an aerial cable car, 1,500 feet above the tall trees. On the way, a bird's-eye view is gained of the Katoomba Falls on one side, and the Jamieson Valley on the other. Another experience out of the ordinary is to dine in the Skyway Restaurant. With a seating capacity of 200, the restaurant features a moving floor which revolves completely every ten minutes, and gives diners passing views of Katoomba Falls, the Three Sisters, the Jamieson Valley, and Malaita Point.

Then there are pony bush trips through the mountains. Sturdy, reliable stock horses, used to the terrain, travel into the real bushland. The guides are true Australian stockmen, and all meals are cooked in campfire fashion. The trails provide easy, comfortable access to fastnesses where native flowers and shrubs, towering trees and wild life, abound.

Until the year 1832, the descent from the summit of the Blue Mountains at Mount York to the recently-discovered Bathurst Plains was a nightmare that came true for every drover, pioneer and bullock-driver edging his way down the precipitous pass. There was, however, one compensation. At the foot of the descent stood an inn with a reputation for comfort, cleanliness and good management that gained the tavern-keeper fame throughout the colony. Clean linen, snow-white napery, sparkling glass and silverware, and roaring log fires, awaited the tired and weary travellers. Three Governors—Bourke, Darling and Macquarie—slept at the inn at various times, and they agreed that, the 'liquors and cuisine were equal to anything in Sydney Town'.

The tavern-keeper, Pierce Collits, arrived in Sydney as a convict in the transport *Minorca* in 1801. His wife came with him as a free woman, and three years later Governor King gave her a grant of seventy acres on the Nepean River. Collits soon earned his conditional pardon and joined his wife on the property, where he became a respected and prosperous farmer. Mrs Collits opened a local school where she taught the settlers' children; and in 1820 Pierce became a government official, being 'Constable, Pound-keeper, and Inspector of Cattle on the Nepean River'.

Pierce Collits was an ambitious man and realized that with the opening of the road over the Blue Mountains travellers would need rest and refreshment, particularly at the end of the terrible plunge down the western face of Mount York. And so, in 1823, he moved to the foot of the pass with his wife and nine children, and proceeded to make a start with his inn. Wagon-loads of furniture, building materials, and provisions were carried over the mountains from Sydney for the new tavern which, when it opened its doors, was called the *Golden Fleece*. However, the proprietor's personality was so strong that his establishment was much better known as *Collits' Inn*. Soon after it opened, the *Sydney Gazette* announced the 'pleasing intelligence' that the journey across the Blue Mountains had shed many of its terrors. 'The good humour and hospitality of the host of the Golden Fleece will tend much to smooth the rugged asperities of the way,' said the newspaper's correspondent after sampling the bill of fare.

The following year, an English visitor of note declared that he had eaten a dinner there as good as that in any London tavern. There were choice steaks, fine wines, delicious sweets and the very best cream and butter. He remarked on the beautiful furniture, and the 'Dutch cleanliness of the kitchen'; and was impressed with the attention given to his horses, whose chafed backs were carefully rubbed with salt water. 'Collits' Inn,' he said, 'is as warm, comfortable and commodious inside as it is picturesque and beautiful without.'

Collits had been granted fifty acres for his tavern; and he also retained his farm on the Nepean, where convict overseers looked after his herd of 200 cattle, his horses, and his crops of grain. In 1824 he petitioned Governor Brisbane for another 200 acres near the inn, pleading his 'unsullied character', his large family, and the public benefit derived from his hostelry. His application was more than successful; it was not only granted in full, but the Governor bestowed another 150 acres on his eldest son, John.

Collits' Inn was now a regular overnight stopping place for the passengers carried on the mail coaches, and its proprietor prospered exceedingly. His farm was doing well, his herds were increasing, and another of his sons, James, was given a grant of 640 acres by Governor Darling as a mark of official favour. There was a black cloud showing, however. As more and more settlers crossed the mountains they complained about the frightful Mount York descent and clamoured for a better road to the west. Collits's son James surveyed an easier route, one that would still bring travellers to the door of his father's inn but it was not adopted. Surveyor-General Thomas Mitchell decided to abandon the Mount York route completely, and official approval was given to a new road—the present Victoria Pass Road—down to Little Hartley.

Pierce Collits remained at Mount York for another two

years, but his famous inn was practically deserted. He petitioned the Governor, and was given an allotment of land at Little Hartley, on his undertaking to build a new inn there. The new tavern was an imposing one; but by this time Hartley was a flourishing centre, and there were five other inns in opposition. Although he was successful, Pierce Collits's day of fame was over.

The Australian musical play, 'Collits' Inn', was based on the legend concerning the daughter Amelia Collits; in the musicale, the name was changed to Mary Collits. The story goes that Amelia, youngest daughter of Pierce, and a charming girl, loved her father's bushranging friend. One day, as the two men played cards in the tap-room of the bar, Amelia saw the redcoats coming, and warned the bushranger, who fled up Mount York to his hide-out in a cave. The redcoats, commanded by Ensign Lake, an English officer, made the inn their headquarters. The officer fell in love with Amelia, but she refused to marry him.

Kitty, the kitchen-maid, became jealous and sent a message to the bushranger saying that Amelia was flirting with Ensign Lake. Filled with anger, the bushranger left his hiding place and came to the inn, where he challenged Lake to a duel. The redcoat won the fight, mortally wounding his opponent.

The grief-stricken Amelia spurned the victor and vowed to marry the first man to come into the tap-room. He was John Skeen, a 77-year-old settler. Two years after their marriage he died; and Ensign Lake, who had returned to England, again came to Australia to win Amelia's heart. But again she refused him.

The little family cemetery is fenced in at the foot of Mount York. Pierce Collits and his wife; a daughter, Mary, who was drowned as a child in the flood waters of the Nepean River; and John Skeen and his wife, are all buried there. Amelia, who was about eighty-four years of age when she died, had no headstone to her grave as the others did, for she was the last of the family.

THIRTEEN

Edward Hargraves

IT was in the early Autumn of 1851 that, as the fortunes and future of the colony of New South Wales swung in the balance, there came the official announcement of the discovery of gold in the Bathurst district—the first discovery of gold in Australia. Over the Blue Mountains and into the virgin bushland, settlers and gold-seekers, storekeepers and adventurers, went by the thousand. They all partook of the spirit of adventure, the lust for freedom, and the lure of the good earth that was opening up the western frontier of the colony.

Day after day the Sydney *Herald* did its best to stop the mad infatuation, the golden obsession that had set in; but all in vain. The 'aureate hopes men set their hearts upon' had proved too much for common sense. The *Herald* correspondent at Bathurst, writing on 20 May, reported:

'The business of the town is utterly paralysed. A complete mental madness appears to have seized every member of the community, and there has been a universal rush to the diggings . . . People of all trades, callings, and pursuits are being quickly transformed into miners, and many a hand trained to wield nothing heavier than the grey goose-quill has become nervous to clutch the pick and crow-bar . . . The blacksmiths cannot turn out picks fast enough . . . the roads to Summer Hill Creek have become literally alive with new-made miners from every quarter, some with picks, others shouldering shovels, and a few strung round with wash-hand basins, tin pots, and colanders, while garden and agricultural implements of every variety either hang from saddle bow or dangle about the persons of the pilgrims . . . Such is the intensity of the excitement that people seem regardless of comfort and think only of gold . . .'

Bathurst, of course, was close to the diggings—shortly afterwards to be named 'Ophir'. Despite the fact that it was impossible in the early days to keep any record of the gold won from the district's fields, it has been possible to estimate fairly accurately the value of the gold obtained, at four-and-a-half million dollars. Within five months of the Ophir discovery, a total of 12,186 held miners' licenses, of which 2,100 were issued at Ophir itself.

Shortly afterwards came the electrifying news of gold being found on land known as 'The Wentworth', a property owned by William Charles Wentworth. This was the origin of Lucknow, a richer field than Ophir. A rough, rustic bridge had been built over a creek, with a deck of poles covered with earth. A girl was crossing the bridge when she noticed something glittering, and picked it up. She showed it to a Dr Favell, who pronounced it to be gold; and Lucknow was born.

Edward Hargraves is credited with being the first to discover payable gold, and so start the dramatic rush which transformed Australia, in three years, from a quiet pastoral backwater to a teeming land of fortune-seekers who would launch a $1600 million industry; one which will yield many millions more in the years to come. Hargraves was by no means the first to find gold in Australia. As early as 1814, convict workers on the road to Bathurst found considerable quantities of it, but were threatened with flogging if they revealed their discovery. Eleven years later a convict was flogged for having in his possession a nugget of gold which he declared he had found in the bush. And in 1839 the Polish nobleman, Paul Strzelecki, found gold in the Vale of Clwydd. It was hardly possible to reward the distinguished explorer with a whipping, but Governor Gipps did the next best thing, and persuaded him to keep the discovery secret.

A strange story is that of the association of Edward Hargraves and his partners—John Lister, and William and James Toms—

who actually found the gold. Hargraves was a pastoralist at Bathurst; but because of droughts and floods he disposed of his property and, in 1848, sailed for the Californian gold-diggings. There he had little success, but he became more and more convinced that he had left behind him in Australia country of a similar nature, which was gold-bearing.

Hargraves returned in 1851, to confirm his belief. He commenced prospecting in the Macquarie district; and when he became lost in a gully, he found his way to Guyong, between Bathurst and Orange. The inn at Guyong was kept by Mrs Lister, and the prospector asked her if she knew of a guide who would accompany him on his prospecting search. She suggested her sixteen-year-old son; and two other youths, William and James Toms, to look after the horses. And so the party set out.

For some time they searched for gold, Hargraves teaching his young assistants the use of the cradle, and imparting other necessary knowledge. On 12 February the trio set out, following a tributary of Summer Hill Creek, itself a tributary of the Macquarie River. 'After travelling about fifteen miles I found myself in the country that I was so anxiously longing to behold again,' Hargraves wrote in his journal.

'The resemblance of its formation to that of California could not be doubted or mistaken. I took the pick and scratched the gravel off a schistose dyke which ran across the creek at right angles with its side; and with a trowel I dug a panful of earth, which I washed in the waterhole. The first trial produced a little piece of gold . . . I then washed five panfuls in succession, obtaining gold from all but one.'

Confirming this discovery by further sampling of creek gravel over an area of seventy by forty miles in the Macquarie valley—including the Turon River, where a vast fortune in gold was to be uncovered in the next few months—Hargraves hastened back to Sydney. There he proposed to bargain with the authorities before he disclosed the auriferous localities. He obtained an interview with the Colonial Secretary, Deas Thomson, who told him that he must trust the Government's generosity after he had named the localities. Hargraves agreed;

and with the Government Geologist returned to Summer Hill Creek where the official soon confirmed the claim.

Hargraves received a Government reward of £500, and later —when the full value of his discovery to Australia was apparent—he received another grant of £10,000. In 1855, the Victorian Parliament voted him a grant of £2,400, and he was engaged later by the Western Australian Government to seek possible goldfields in that State. He missed the rich areas of Kalgoorlie and Coolgardie, however, and his search was a failure. Hargraves eventually settled down on a farm in the Hawkesbury district, and was given a State pension. At about the time of his death in 1891, considerable publicity was given to claims by the youth who had accompanied him on his first trip, John Lister, and the brothers William and James Toms, that they, and not Hargraves, were the first real discoverers of payable gold. Representatives of Lister contended that he took Hargraves to the historic spot; and the Toms brothers claimed that they were the first men to get gold in payable quantities.

Eventually the New South Wales Assembly appointed a select committee to investigate the allegations. Lister died before his evidence could be taken, but a statement he had written was accepted. The committee's finding was an extraordinary one. They decided that the claimants were undoubtedly the first actual discoverers of payable gold, although Hargraves had taught them the use of the pan and cradle, and other proper methods of searching for the metal. Considering that in the absence of this technical knowledge, none of the claimants could have found the metal in payable quantities, and that the evidence was taken forty years after the event, it seems a strange verdict.

FOURTEEN

Southern Highlands

A BROAD col in the vicinity of Goulburn separates the rugged mountain area south of the Blue Mountains from the more mature Monaro plateau and the eastern slopes of the Australian Alps. Known as the Southern Highlands of New South Wales, the region covers more than a thousand square miles of lofty plateau country. The landscapes of the Southern Highlands are made up in large measure of timber-clad ranges which run east and south from the Wombeyan Caves to within full view of the Pacific Ocean. Primaeval rainforest is to be found in these ranges, and fern-trees line the steep gorges into which mountain streams plunge hundreds of feet; but in the open country rich, gently-sloping farmlands merge with the resort townships.

Main roads and tree-shaped byways lead to such attractions as historic Berrima Village, Fitzroy Falls, Wombeyan Caves, Kangaroo Valley, the Belmore and Carrington Falls, Tallong Look-out and Mount Cambewarra. Big wildlife parks and sanctuaries complement virgin forests with splendid valley and summit views. These bushland parks include the 50,000-acre Morton National Park which surrounds the Fitzroy Falls, the Robertson Wildlife Refuge, and the Tallowa Sanctuary.

Approached from Sydney via the Hume Highway, which passes through the historic towns of Camden and Picton, the Southern Highlands proper begin in the fertile Braemar-Mittagong country, some seventy-odd miles from Sydney. The approach from the south is through the city of Goulburn, a big stock and wool market, and the largest centre between Sydney and Canberra. The Highlands, with a resident population of around 23,000, support a variety of farming and commercial industries. Rich grazing lands for sheep, and for stud beef and dairy cattle, and thoroughbred horse studs, are intermingled with stone and pome fruit orchards, and much vegetable cultivation. The district has a wealth of coal, trachyte, limestone, sandstone and building marble. Mittagong, the site of the now long-defunct Fitzroy Ironworks, established in 1848, has the honour of being the birthplace of the vital Australian iron-and-steel industry.

The Southern Highlands were first explored as early as 1798 by John Wilson, a remarkable individual, who was in turn convict, explorer and 'wild white man' (he lived for a time among the Aborigines). A few years later, in 1802, Francis Barrallier of the New South Wales Corps—whose name is commemorated in a village in the region—came south to the Picton district, in an attempt to by-pass the Blue Mountains. The following year John Macarthur received the grant of land at Camden on which his famous woolgrowing experiments were carried out.

In 1814, the country south of Camden was rediscovered and explored by Hamilton Hume, after whom the Hume Highway is named; then Governor Macquarie saw the region on his southern journey in 1820. Settlement proceeded steadily after Hume's explorations, and throughout the nineteenth century. Early settlers in the district included two of Australia's most important explorers, John Oxley and Captain Sturt. Most of the old and beautifully-tended rural properties, now such a delight to the eye of the visitor, were carved out of the dense but intensely fertile 'brush country' in the pioneering days. Lonely outposts like Mittagong, Bowral and Moss Vale emerged as thriving towns that straddled the trade routes from Sydney to the Riverina and Victoria.

The quiet little village of Robertson stands on the edge of a mountain range 2,400 feet above sea level. The village is surrounded by pleasant dairying and pastoral country, and an English touch is given to the landscape by the hills and hedges, and trees with a foliage of dark green. Macquarie Pass, which leads down the mountain from Robertson, affords views of Lake Illawarra and the Pacific Ocean, and of various south-coast towns. The Macquarie Falls are close to the pass, while a natural pulpit at Carrington Falls looks out over another fine panorama.

Robertson was the first area settled under Sir John Robertson's controversial 1861 Land Act, which gave settlers the right to obtain a grant of land provided they cleared it of the almost impenetrable semi-tropical vegetation. The Robertson Natural Park—of which the Robertson Wildlife Refuge is a part—is a good illustration of the difficulties the pioneers had to face with axe and saw. The Wildlife Refuge, a virgin rainforest, is one of the few remaining sizeable stands of the original thick forest growth common in Australia's pre-settlement days. The primitiveness of the refuge is largely intact, although a number of walking paths have been introduced. Many fine specimens of rainforest softwoods may be seen—corkwood, sassafras, lilli-pilli, coachwood—and there is prolific birdlife, particularly satin bowerbirds, whip birds and wonga pigeons.

Bundanoon is a pleasant spot on the verge of the plateau overlooking mountain and gorge country of the Kangaroo and Shoalhaven River valleys. The little township called Bundanoon (an Aboriginal word meaning 'big, deep gullies') has a deal of charm, with its avenues of trees and its superb setting. Winding bushland trails and wildlife sanctuaries are contained in the surrounding mountain country, where may be seen the Grand Canyon, the Amphitheatre, and the fern-edged pools of Fairy Bower and Glow Worm Glen. Here, too, are heard the vibrant calls of the lyre-bird—the 'native pheasant', as it was known to the early settlers.

When the region was first explored in 1798 by John Wilson, 'the wild white man', he produced the first known specimen of the lyre-bird, calling it a 'native pheasant'. The bird is nearly the sole survivor of a very ancient race of beings. The distance of the lineage is indicated by the primitive character of certain small bones around the eyes. These are found in only a few other species, all descended from ancient types.

Artists who made pioneer attempts to depict the lyre-bird

with its noble tail displayed, were about as near to Nature as modern delineators of the bird in display attitude. The lyre-tail is not carried as shown in these pictures, and the mistake has been perpetuated in stamp designs. There is some excuse for these artists, since it is difficult to depict the tail as it actually appears when the bird is performing on his dancing mound, or elsewhere. Even a clear photograph conveys but a general idea of the bird's pose and of the appearance of the tail, over which its owner has perfect control. When starting to dance, the bird does sometimes hold his tail nearly upright, but not so as to form a conventional lyre. The characteristic manner of displaying brings the tail into action. It is vibrated until the filmy feathers, swung over the performer's head, becomes misty to the sight, while the ornamented lyre-feathers, depressed with the others, are carried outspread. The lyre-bird delights in rhythmic movements, and when performing on the mound may advance and retreat as if Nature had taught him the steps of some Dawntime dance.

The historic village of Berrima is a 'must' for any visitor to the Southern Highlands. Its site was selected in 1829 by Major (later Sir) Thomas Mitchell, the then Surveyor-General of New South Wales, who was planning the line of a new road south to avoid the steep ascent of the Mittagong Range. The word Berrima was the Aboriginal name of the locality. Mitchell selected the site because there were already a number of settlers nearby, and because plenty of building material was available locally as well as a pure and abundant water-supply from the Wingecarribee River.

Mitchell was responsible for the town planning, which was approved by Governor Darling in 1831. The Court House was completed in 1838; it was used as a court for the last time in 1900, and is now the Berrima School of Arts. The Berrima Gaol was completed in 1839, being enlarged in 1866 (the date inscribed over the entrance); it was closed as a gaol in 1909, used as an internment camp in World War I, and then remained virtually unused until, after remodelling, it was opened in 1949 as a training centre for the rehabilitation of young prisoners.

The foundation stone of the Church of Holy Trinity was laid in 1847 by Bishop Broughton, the architect being Edmund

Blacket, 'the Christopher Wren of Australia', who designed the main building of the University of Sydney, St Andrew's Cathedral and many other well-known churches in New South Wales. In 1849 Archbishop Polding laid the foundation stone of the Catholic Church at Berrima, which was completed two years later.

The *Surveyor-General Inn*, named after Major Mitchell, is the oldest continuously licensed inn in Australia still trading within its original walls. Its first licence was granted to James Harper on 29 June, 1835. (Tasmania's *Bush Inn* at New Norfolk is ten years older, but there have been some architectural changes in the original building.)

Berrima is a purely Australian type of village, not modelled on the pattern of English or other villages, but built of local materials to suit local conditions. Here is an authentic segment of the early history of Australia strikingly revealed in the beautiful sandstone buildings of the village. Symbolic in its way of Australia's drive to nationhood, and of the courage, hopes, energy and hardships of the pioneers—and symbolic, too, perhaps, of a certain rugged lawlessness in the country's past— the colonial village of Berrima is unique in Australia, and needs to be jealously preserved. As time passes, the risk grows that historic buildings will be allowed to fall into ruin, or be pulled down to make way for the new, unless steps are taken to preserve them. In recognition of this, the Berrima Village Trust was set up in April 1963 to preserve Berrima as a colonial village. The aim of the trust is to protect and preserve all lands and buildings in Berrima which are of beauty, or of national, historical, cultural or other interest; and to provide, maintain and improve amenities and access to them.

Bowral, at the foot of Mount Gibraltar which stands sentinel-like over the amphitheatre in which the township is built, is noted for its parks and gardens and its English style of countryside. Like other places on the Southern Highlands, Bowral is a popular health resort, and its bracing climate has encouraged the establishment of a number of private schools there. Many well-known stud-cattle properties, including the King Ranch, are located in the district; while the renowned

Bowral Horse Show, held in early January each year, attracts horse-lovers from far afield. Massed displays of tulips are to be seen in the parks and gardens of Bowral during its annual Tulip Time Festival, and it is during this time that the Bong Bong picnic race-meeting is held. Crowds of both city and country dwellers make a real social occasion of the day, and of the ball at night.

The Bong Bong and other picnic races are part of Australia's bush tradition, and evolved in the days when country people were cut off from each other by great distances. Picnic race-meetings were a means of foregathering, and are an historical part of Australia's early social life. Nowadays streamlined cars and private planes have replaced bullock waggons and sulkies for the conveyance of guests, but the old atmosphere and lavish hospitality remain.

At all these picnic race-meetings, the usual week's festivities embraced racing, pigeon shoots, kangaroo shoots, and a day set aside for children's sports. Each day's activities would be followed by a dance at night, which went on well into the early hours of the next day. The guests brought their own camping equipment and food—all except meat, which was supplied by the station-owner host.

A feature of picnic races which seems to have remained the same throughout the years is the fun of the accommodation problem. At the annual meetings country pubs take the over-flow of guests from the homesteads. As many as six visitors often have to share one bedroom, and a method of providing hanging space for the clothes is to tie a rope from wall to wall. Elegant race frocks and glamorous evening gowns hanging on a rope among the homely furnishings of a small bush pub make an incongruous picture.

The first recorded picnic race meeting was in the 1830s on Dr Gibson's property, 'Tirranna', in the Goulburn district. Guests arrived for lunch, and after the races were entertained at dinner and a ball at the homestead. The picnic day was a picnic in name only. The meal menus were in the nature of banquets, with champagne flowing, and the women guests wore their finest imported model gowns. During heavy rains one year, just before the picnic races, the 'Tirranna' property

Cave formations give the Blue Mountains a living vividness,
startlingly grand and often awesome (page 89)

Tumut Ponds Dam, helping to store the waters of the Snowy River (page 118)

Guthega Dam—part of the Snowy Mountains Hydro-Electric Scheme (page 117)

was flooded, and one of their most promising mounts was housed in the big drawing-room, lest the animal should be swept away by the flood.

By 1871 the 'Tirranna' race-meeting had become so popular with city visitors, as well as with country guests, that it was decided by a committee to thank Dr and Mrs Gibson for performing the arduous task of entertaining so many people, and to make a ruling that in future guests should provide their own lunches and dinners. The ball, which had outgrown the 'Tirranna' ball-room, was to be held in the township of Goulburn.

In the meantime, picnic race-meetings had been established on other country properties in New South Wales, Victoria and Queensland.

Goulburn is the commercial centre of the Southern Highlands although it is, strictly speaking, outside the region. It is within easy distance of the Wombeyan Caves, which are remarkable for the beauty and delicacy of their limestone formations. Here, in immense cathedral-like caverns, the ceaseless dripping of limestone-impregnated water has created, over tens of thousands of years, a subterranean wonderland of miniature forests and walled cities, frozen cascades and water-falls, tinted marble walls and strange sculptures. Many absorbing hours can be spent in examining the bushland reserve surrounding the caves, where wildflowers and wildlife are protected.

Moss Vale, on the Highland Way, is the centre of a pleasant rural district, with an invigorating climate and a great deal of attractive scenery. As with Bowral and Mittagong, early settlers around Moss Vale planted English trees and shrubs which are still a feature of the district. The deciduous trees make springtime a joy, and the evergreens maintain their glory all year round. Many beautiful homes may be seen in and around Moss Vale. Historic 'Throsby Park', one of the earliest homes, is open for inspection on occasions, and is being preserved by the National Trust. The one-time country residence of the State Governor is at nearby Sutton Forest.

The town of Mittagong nestles in the valley of the Nattai

River near its source, beneath the rocky buttress of Mount Gibraltar and the wooded slopes of Mount Alexander. A drive over 'the range' and Mount Gibraltar reveals the district's many landscape attractions; and even a few minutes walk from the town provides much of scenic interest. About one-and-a-half miles from Mittagong are the Sixty Feet Falls, which cascade with graceful effect over the mountainside; Lake Alexandra, just ten minutes' walk from the town, is a place of charm; and Mount Alexandra often provides a magnificent display of wildflowers.

The ideal time to visit Mount Alexandra is in November, when the slopes are lit with the glowing blooms of the waratah, the floral emblem of New South Wales. Here, surely, the legend of the waratah was enacted and here, for the first time, the following story was told by the Aboriginal song-maker and teller of tales:

In the Dreamtime there lived a beautiful girl called Krubi. She made for herself a cloak of the red skin of the rock wallaby and had it ornamented with the still brighter crests of the gang-gang cockatoo.

Now, Krubi loved a young and brave warrior and every day from a cleft between two great sandstone rocks she would watch for his return from the hunt. As the tribe of hunters returned each day, the red figure was the first object to strike their eyes. The young man, Camoola, looked for that cloak alone, and would run to greet the girl.

But one day Krubi's heart was filled with sorrow, for as she stood on the ridge she heard from afar the fierce cries of battle, and occasionally glimpsed the sight of swaying crowds of warriors. At dusk she watched for their return, but no young figure stepped out eagerly from the victors to greet her. For days she stayed there waiting and hoping, and then in her sorrow, with the power that all Aborigines possess, she willed herself to die.

In death she passed into the most majestic of Australian flowers—the waratah. The stalk is firm and straight, without a blemish: just like the man Krubi died for. The leaves are serrated and have points just like his spears, and the glorious flower is red—redder and more glowing than any other in this land—signifying Krubi's everlasting love.

In a secluded mountain valley fourteen miles from Mittagong is the 'ghost town' of Joadja, whose former prosperity was not founded on gold but on shale oil. Slowly but surely the bush is reclaiming the clearings, and covering fallen buildings and ruined houses. Oddly enough, the native trees and shrubs are not alone in this task, for the long-departed dwellers beautified their township with English trees—including elms, poplars and sycamores—which have flourished to an extent little imagined by those who planted them.

Joadja is on a private property but it has recently been opened for inspection by supervised parties; a per capita charge is levied, the money being used for restoration purposes. Here was produced the richest shale oil in Australia, and here in this quiet valley many products such as gasolene, kerosene, lubricating oils, candles, waxes and soaps, were manufactured from the shale.

Edward Carter, a member of a pastoralist family in the Mittagong district, discovered Joadja's shale deposits in 1850. An area of 1,944 acres was taken over by the Australian Kerosene Oil and Mineral Company Limited to exploit the deposits, and much capital was invested. A model town was laid out with streets of neat brick cottages, shops, hotels, a post-office and a theatre. It even boasted one of the first telephone services in the colony. The company built its own private railway line connecting Joadja with Mittagong, so linking it with Sydney and elsewhere, and the shale workings were served with tramways, which also operated a haulage system up the mountainside. The latest mining mechanism was installed, including the first mechanical coal-cutter to be used in New South Wales.

Several of the mine managers and many of the workmen were Scotsmen who, together with their families, had been brought out by the company. A large orchard was planted near the main offices, and this was protected by a windbreak of Norfolk Island pines. The now fully grown trees are flourishing, and the orchard still bears a profusion of apples, pears, peaches and nectarines, upon which the birds of the district feast.

The main street, Carrington Row, is grass-grown, and gum-trees are growing through the roofs of what were once imposing buildings. The roof of the Town Hall has fallen in, the post-office is in ruins, and the hotels are but empty shells. The dawn of the twentieth century saw the beginning of the end for Joadja. Production fell off rapidly with the thinning-out of the shale seams, and in 1906 the company went into voluntary liquidation, so ending Joadja's brief industrial existence.

FIFTEEN

Mystery Lake

DIVERGING from the Great Dividing Range at Lake George, and extending northwards, is a low mountain-system in New South Wales known as the Cullarin Range (sometimes spelled Cullerin). Its northern boundary is uncertain, one authority considering that it extends as far as the Liverpool Range and includes the main dividing range, while others place its northernmost limit near Crookwell. The Cullarin Range includes several elevations of more than 3,000 feet, the highest point in the more limited area being Mount McAlister (3,388 feet). The Sydney-Melbourne railway crosses the range at Cullerin station, about twenty miles west of Goulburn. Near Lake George, the name given to a basin in the Cullarin Range, the Mundoonen Range branches out on the west.

Lake George is Australia's will-o'-the-wisp. Sometimes a stormy inland sea which has caused several tragedies, sometimes a stretch of dry grazing land, it has mystified settlers and scientists for nearly a century. Boats and cars have been raced over the same course on this disappearing lake. It covers an area of about sixteen miles in length and six miles in width, with a twenty-five foot depth of water. When the lake vanishes, the rich pasture of its bed—valued by holders of adjoining land—covers 38,500 acres.

When the first white men came to this district, in about 1812, the lake was described as 'a vast sheet of water, stretching southwards as far as the eye could see, whose billows were rolling in upon the foothills as the veritable billows of the ocean—if it were not part of the Pacific itself'. The first explorers were told by Aborigines that the lake was covered with a forest but all the water disappeared through the bottom. To them it was known as Werriwa. In October 1820 Governor Macquarie visited the lake and named it after King George IV.

In 1843 the lake was quite dry and remained so until 1852, when it filled again. It was recorded that there were thousands of black swans on the lake, and that the waters teemed with fish; yet by 1870 it was dry again. After the lake first disappeared many pioneers settled on the rich soil along the slopes of the lake-bed. They prospered for a number of years; but then, just as mysteriously as it had vanished, the lake began to make its appearance again. Soon waves were lapping around the fences of the homesteads, and the farms had to be abandoned. Before long the homes were entirely under water, and the lake became renowned for the great cod caught there. It is a remarkable feature that large fish appeared in the waters soon after it filled.

A rather extensive report on Lake George was made in 1887. It was then disclosed that the lake was situated at the summit of the Great Dividing Range, 2,230 feet above sea-level. The Government Astronomer of the time described it as the largest and most important freshwater lake in the colony.

In about 1900, the lake began to disappear again; and there was no water at all by 1902. Wonderful crops of tomatoes and other vegetables were grown on the lake-bed; but settlers were cautious, and only used the rich grasslands for grazing. They were wise—very wise. By 1925 Lake George was again a big sheet of water with yachtsmen, swimmers and game-hunters enjoying these sports at their best.

In the 1930s, the lake completely dried up; twenty years later it was again a very beautiful sheet of water, at times storm-tossed and menacing. The mystery of where the water goes to has never been solved satisfactorily. Geologists cannot agree; they say that evaporation could not possibly remove so many millions of gallons in the few years which are sufficient for the lake's disappearance. Plenty of theories have been put forward but none can be proved. One view is that artesian bores far away in Central Australia drain the lake in dry seasons.

Undoubtedly the lake is the crater of a volcano which has not been active for scores of thousands of years. A likely theory is that earth tremors, which are often felt in the district, open up fissures in the bed, allowing the waters to drain into subterranean rivers. Perhaps, some day, another fault in the earth's structure will give way, and reveal underground channels that will explain the mystery.

Nevertheless, all these theories fail to account for the large fish that have appeared in the lake almost immediately after it fills. It seems that Lake George will remain Australia's mystery lake, possibly the only place in the world where sculling and motor car races have taken place over the same course.

Not far from Lake George is the historic *Collector Hotel*, on the road to Canberra. The hotel was the scene of epic events in the bushranging days, and it now contains a museum of convict and bushranging relics. Outside the building is a granite monument marking the spot where Constable Nelson (the father of eight children) was shot dead by the nineteen-year-old bushranger, John Dunn. On 26 January, 1865, Ben Hall, John Gilbert, and Dunn—who had teamed up with the other two the previous year—rode into the village of Collector, and stuck up the hotel. Hall and Gilbert entered the hotel, and left young Dunn on guard outside. Constable Nelson came down the road when told that bushrangers were in town, and Dunn shot him as he approached.

The trio were proclaimed outlaws, and a few months later the police surrounded Ben Hall in the bush near Forbes and shot him. Gilbert was shot by the police at the home of Thomas Kelly, Dunn's grandfather. Dunn escaped, but was caught later and hanged. It was generally believed that both Hall and Gilbert had been betrayed; hence the verses of later years, containing the lines:

> The smallest child on the Watershed
> Can tell you how Gilbert died.

Bell Hall was the boldest of all the bushrangers, and he stirred the imagination of the whole country with his daring escapades. He was aged twenty-eight at the time of his death;

and when his body was carted into Forbes on a pack-horse, 500 people lined the streets in silent mourning. And the balladists sang:

> Come all Australia's sons to me,
> A hero has been slain;
> Butchered by cowards in his sleep,
> Upon the Lachlan Plain . . .

In the wild colonial days, it was only a short step from cattle-stealing to bushranging. Some of the bushrangers were the sons of local farmers, well-known to all the people around. There was no need for these men to hide from the police troopers in inaccessible mountain caves; they could seek shelter among their friends all round the country. Often the whole countryside was in league with them, and the coming of police was made known to them miles away. When the troopers arrived, they would search for their quarry in vain.

Force of circumstances, rather than intent, drove many of these outlaws to a life of crime. Ben Hall was one such example. He was a young boy when his parents died, and he was befriended by a squatter named Hamilton who gave the lad his first job. Hamilton grew very fond of young Ben, finding that he possessed great ability as a stockman; and it was not long before he made him the station manager. Within a few years, Ben Hall had saved up enough money to buy a station of his own and to marry the daughter of a squatter named Walsh. The marriage was his downfall, for the girl was unworthy of him; it seemed that everyone in the district was aware of her reputation—except Ben himself. One day when he returned from a cattle muster, he found his wife had run off with a man named Taylor and had left a note worded as follows:

'Ben, my boy, try and forget me. I love a scoundrel—yes I admit he is a scoundrel—but I love him. That is if love be the word. Infatuation? Call it what you wish. Taylor has destroyed my duty to you as a wife, and I have destroyed your happiness for life.
Something was in me that I had not fortitude to resist. I hope, however, that you will have sufficient manliness to bear up against the conduct of a worthless woman. Don't

follow me. You have always been too good a man for me. Two villains are more suitable for each other, possessing no conscience nor even the fear of God or the devil.

Good-bye Ben.'

The letter was a tremendous shock to Ben Hall. For fifteen days he rode about the countryside like a madman, hardly knowing what he was doing, and getting mixed up in dubious company. He was unlucky enough to be camping with some cattle-thieves when they were arrested, and although he was later discharged, he became so embittered that he turned bushranger.

Ben Hall's teenager assistant, John Dunn, is buried in Bunnerong Cemetery, at Botany Bay. A woman claimed the young bushranger's body after the hanging at Darlinghurst Jail, arranged for the burial and the erection of a tombstone on the grave. The inscription reads:

He has gone to his grave, but we must not deplore him,
Though sorrow and darkness encompass his tomb;
The Saviour has passed through its portals before him,
And the light of His love was the lamp through his gloom.

Inside the *Collector Hotel* museum can be seen the blood-stained couch on which Constable Nelson's body was placed after the shooting by Dunn. There is a fine set of pewter mugs, more than a century old, from which the Ben Hall gang drank, while cat-o'-nine tails, leg-irons, handcuffs and a flogging horse—all of which were used for the punishment of convicts stationed in the district—are part of the exhibits.

SIXTEEN

Colossus of Water and Mortar

THE Great Dividing Range is vital to the life of the Australian people. The major part of the mainland lies in the dry belt which encircles the Southern Hemisphere between fifteen and thirty-five degrees south latitude. Except for the northern fringe of the continent, its northern areas are too far south to benefit fully from the monsoonal downpours of the wet Tropics, and its southern areas too far to the north to receive the regular rains of the Temperate Zone. Thus, geographical position is coupled with the limited extent of mountain ranges and the effect of high annual evaporation loss to render Australia the world's driest continent.

The average annual rainfall over the mainland is only sixteen-and-a-half inches, compared with an average of twenty-six inches for all the land surfaces of the world. The total annual run-off to the sea is equivalent to a depth of water spread over the mainland of only one-and-a-third inches, compared with nine inches for the United States of America, and nine-and-three-quarter inches for all land areas of the world. The total annual flow of all Australian rivers is only about half that of the Mississippi.

It is vital, therefore, that full use be made of the country's meagre water resources. And this is being achieved in the Snowy Mountains Scheme, which is not only a colossus of water and mortar, but represents much more. It is a monument to Australian know-how; it is the answer to the pessimist; it is a national pride of achievement. Rivers that ran to waste—waters lost to the sea for timeless aeons—are now harnessed for the nation's prosperity by one of man's boldest projects in water and power development. Here men have moved and rebuilt mountains; they have broken wild mountain rivers and raging streams, diverting them into a hundred miles of tremendous under-mountain tunnels, cut at startling speeds through solid granite. In places these tunnels are thousands of feet below the summit of the peaks. The scheme is one of the largest engineering achievements the world has known, and it must be seen to be believed.

The most reliable source of water on the Australian mainland is that part of the Great Dividing Range known as the Snowy Mountains, lying in south-eastern New South Wales and north-eastern Victoria. Remnants of an ancient alpine range, the Snowy Mountains, are snow-covered for about six months each year, and give rise to three great river systems—the Murray and Murrumbidgee rivers, flowing westward, and the Snowy River, rising on the eastern slopes and flowing in the opposite direction, to the south-eastern coast.

The Murray and Murrumbidgee rivers flow for hundreds of miles across dry but otherwise fertile plains to the coast of South Australia. Irrigation is already well-established on these plains, but further large-scale expansion is dependent upon the supply of more water. On the other hand, the Snowy River flows through an area with reliable and adequate rainfall to waste itself in the nearby Tasman Sea.

Not only are the waters of the Snowy River considerable in volume, but also they originate at high elevations. By diverting them inland, through huge and lengthy tunnels driven through the Great Dividing Range, these waters can be utilized for the double purpose of producing tremendous quantities of electricity for industry, and of enabling 1,000 square miles of dry land on the western plains to be brought into use for food production.

The Snowy Mountains Scheme embraces an area of more than 2,000 square miles of mountainous country. Contained within a radius of forty miles will be a complex of seventeen major dams and many smaller ones, about 100 miles of tunnels, seven power stations, more than eighty miles of high mountain aqueducts to catch the mountain streams, about 400 miles of power transmission lines, a network of roads, and two new towns.

There is no commercial production of nuclear power in Australia at present but there are prospects of nuclear power stations being established in the future, particularly in areas remote from the coal fields. However, the higher cost of peak-load power compared with the cost of base-load power is even more marked in the case of a nuclear plant than for a coal burning plant. The hydro-electric power station is ideal for the production of peak-load power, and is the logical partner for the nuclear plant. The advantage of the nuclear hydro-electric combination has been proved overseas; the Snowy Mountains Scheme shows that Australia has the resources to develop herself, and so match other progressive countries.

For very many years the potential of the Snowy Mountains has fired the imagination of far-sighted Australians, who realize that their future depends on development. Probably the first white men to see the Snowy River were survivors of the *Sydney Cove*, a vessel outward bound from India to Sydney, and wrecked on the Furneaux Islands in Bass Strait. They crossed the river, close to its mouth, as they made their way around the coast to Sydney.

In 1823 Captain J. M. Currie, R.N., accompanied by Brigade Major Ovens and by Joseph Wild—who had discovered Lake George three years earlier—explored this area as far south as Billilingra, some twelve miles north of the site where Cooma now stands. The following year, explorers Hume and Hovell, on their journey from Yass to Port Phillip, sighted snow-covered peaks which they named 'South Australian Alps', and subsequently referred to as 'snow-mountains'. In 1834 John Lhotsky made a journey to the Australian Alps; he claimed to be the first to bring the name 'Snowy River' to public notice.

When Strzelecki climbed the Main Range in 1840, there were sixty grazing holdings in what is now known as the Snowy River Shire. Indeed, settlement of the western side of the Great Dividing Range had so far advanced that Henry Bingham was appointed as Crown Lands Commissioner at Tumut. Seven years later the village of Cooma was proclaimed. At Cooma, named from an Aboriginal word meaning 'open country', the Head Office of the Snowy Mountains Scheme Authority is located today.

Events leading to the beginning of the Snowy Mountains Scheme can be traced back to 1840 when Strzelecki, in Tasmania, wrote about the possibilities of and need for, irrigation in Australia; as did others, in Victoria especially. This demand was intensified by severe droughts in New South Wales, in the years 1877 and 1878. Giving evidence before a Royal Commission on Water Conservation in 1884, P. F. Adams, Surveyor-General for New South Wales, suggested diverting the Snowy River to the Murrumbidgee. He also suggested that the Tooma River could be diverted to the Murrumbidgee, and put forward the idea that the Snowy water could be stored in Lake George, or diverted to the Lachlan River.

C. E. Blomfield, in 1899, drew attention to the great power potential of the Snowy River; and by 1904, two definite proposals were made for hydro-electric development of the river. Various conferences were held and, as a result, it was decided to build Burrinjuck Dam, and to develop the Murrumbidgee Irrigation Area in New South Wales. In 1939 another severe drought occurred in New South Wales, and Murrumbidgee Irrigation interests fought for the diversion of the Snowy to the Murrumbidgee. This proposal was opposed by interests such as the Snowy River Hydro-electric Development League and the Greater Gippsland League, who wanted to use the Snowy to generate power for the development of the Monaro district and Gippsland.

The first scheme of any magnitude incorporating the dual purpose of irrigation, and of the generation of electricity, was not put forward until 1944. During the Second World War, the vital national need for increasing power supplies and food production again focussed attention on the potential of the Snowy River waters. In the post-war years, further studies were carried out; and in 1947 a Technical Committee representing the Commonwealth and the States of New South Wales and Victoria was set up. Two years later the Snowy Mountains Authority was established. Detailed investigations and construction work by the newly formed Authority started immediately.

Thousands of people make up the working forces of the organization: engineers, surveyors, accountants, dozer-drivers, tunnellers, dam-builders, road-makers and bridge-builders, typists, cooks and waitresses, school teachers and ministers of religion, doctors and nurses: men and women of almost every walk of life—Australians working alongside migrants from thirty different nations—combining all their efforts to complete this inspiring engineering masterpiece. Little wonder that it was listed by the American Society of Civil Engineers, in consultation with National Engineering Societies of other countries, as one of the 'Seven Future Engineering Wonders of the World'.

Fifty-three men have died in the great under-mountain tunnels through which the diverted waters hurtle to turn the wheels of the many power stations. Death is one of the harsh realities of high-speed tunnelling work. It is a tribute the miner must pay for his assault on nature. Misfiring explosives and rock falls have claimed the majority of victims, but strict safety requirements have reduced the deathroll to almost half the average rate in the tunnelling of European Alps.

The construction of the Snowy Scheme is well past the half-way mark, and the last power project is expected to be completed by 1975. The most remarkable feature of the construction has been the rate of progress achieved, particularly in tunnelling. World records for speed in driving big-diameter tunnels through hard granite have been repeatedly broken, the maximum advance at one tunnel face in a six-day week being 541 feet. Even greater speeds have been achieved in driving tunnels of smaller diameter. All major contracts have been completed ahead of time, save one—which was completed on time.

Inseparable from the history of the region is the memory of 'Banjo' Paterson's *Man from Snowy River*.

'He hails from Snowy River, up by Kosciusko side,
Where the hills are twice as steep and twice as rough;
Where a horse's hoofs strike firelight
    from the flint stones every stride,
The man who holds his own is good enough.'

SEVENTEEN

The Roof of Australia

YEARS ago, the writer published an article in the *Sydney Morning Herald*, dealing with 'The White Roof of Australia'. In the article, it was stated that in wintertime the Australian snowfields cover a combined area greater than the whole of Switzerland; and, further, that Australia had the second oldest ski club in the world. This club was formed in the early 1860s, soon after the first ski club was established in Norway; and the article went on to claim that ski-ing was a sport in Australia years before Switzerland had even heard of it.

The following day a worried editor phoned me saying that the office had been 'inundated' with letters and phone-calls from incredulous readers: 'Was I absolutely certain of my statements?' Few Australians of twenty-odd years ago were aware of their wonderful snow heritage, of the perfect ski-ing conditions, or of the alpine grandeur and beauty to be found amidst this country's tranquil mountains. Today all is changed, with luxury hotels, chalets, lodges and alpine villages catering for the thousands of visitors to these snow-mantled mountains.

The enormous snow region has an average altitude of 6,000 feet—the ideal height for ski-ing—and is free from major avalanches, glaciers and other hazards that are so common in the snowfields of Europe. Australian snowfields, from 5,000 to 7,300 feet, are lower than most of those in the Americas and Europe, but they are in many ways superior and safer. Older geographically, the mountains have smooth, curved sides, and some of the slopes have 1,500 to 2,000 feet of ski-running.

There are no ravines nor jagged ridges, few rocks, and most of the ski-ing country is either above the timber line, or very lightly wooded with snow gums. The weather, too, is more temperate than in the snow country of other lands, and temperatures are rarely below zero. The Australian Alps provide snow scenery for upwards of ten months of the year, and skiers have about six months of the year for the practice of their sport over superb snowlands. For several years of late, while England has been hoping in vain for a white Christmas, ski-ing clubs in Australia have held summer races on Christmas Day and Boxing Day.

Mid-winter days in the Australian Alps are very often supremely calm, inviting you to sunbake for hours at a time. To trek in the early morning over the frozen slopes, while the tree shadows are still long and blue, with the crunch of crisp snow beneath one's boots, is to discover a new vigour of thought and being. The shadow-lace of shrub and snow gum, the absolute stillness and silence, are absorbed into one's being.

The snow gums paint the Australian Alps with the glory of their many-hued barks and trunks. Sunlight lends added brilliance to their blues, oranges and pinks; their main background of softer creamy-green hues gaining contrast from the brighter slashes of colour in their bark. The archways, as of cloisters, which they form over a track, blend picturesquely with the gemmed quilt of snow on the path, with its delicately traced pattern of blue shadows from the leafy branches above. Snow gums, well-sheltered from the wind and grown to their full stature, have a grace and elegance unsurpassed in any other Australian tree. Frost-rimed, adorned by snow, they stand motionless in the still air; yet the gentlest wind stirs them into tremulous and glimmering beauty.

A snow gum plays a role in one of my favourite Aboriginal legends—that of the Ice Maidens.

In the Dreamtime, many ages ago, the cluster of stars which we now know as the Pleiades, was formed by seven beautiful ice maidens. Though their home was in the sky, the seven sisters often wandered across the land, bewitching men by their beauty, yet remaining aloof. One day two brothers succeeded in capturing two of the ice maidens. They took them to their camp fire, and endeavoured to melt the cold crystals which surrounded them. They succeeded only in dimming their icy brightness; and despite the fervour of their love, they failed to win the affections of their captives.

The ice maidens were sad and lonely in their captivity, and longed for their home in the sky. At night they could see their five sisters beckoning to them, as they twinkled afar off. One day they were gathering tree bark. They came to a great snow gum, and began to strip the bark from it. As they did so the snow gum (which belonged to the same totem as the ice maidens) extended itself to the sky. The maidens joyfully climbed it to the home of their sisters. But they never regained their original brightness; and that is the reason why there are five bright stars and two dim ones in the group we call the Pleiades.

The two brothers were very grieved at their loss. They laid aside their weapons and mourned for the maidens until the dark hand of death fell on them. Then the gods took pity on the brothers and placed them in the sky, where they could hear the sisters singing. On a starry night you will see those two heavenly bodies, which we now call Orion's Sword and Belt. But the Aborigines remember them as the faithful lovers who have listened to the song of the stars from the birth of time.

The principal snowfields of the Australian mainland are situated in a semi-circular chain of alps, which follow the coastline of the south-eastern portion of the continent, and are in no part of their course much more than one hundred miles distant from the sea. This semi-circle of snow-covered mountains is divided into two unequal sectors by the valley of the Murray River. The smaller Victorian sector contains mountains over 6,000 feet in height, including Mount Hotham, and Mount Feathertop, with Mount Buffalo as its snow terminus.

The larger New South Wales sector runs from near the interstate border to Kiandra, which is the snow terminus on the New South Wales side. It contains the highest peak in Australia, Mount Kosciusko (7,314 feet), and its surrounding plateau; as well as an almost continuous sixty-mile ridge of mountains, including Mount Townsend (7,251 feet), Ramshead (7,197 feet), Mount Gungartan (6,776 feet), and Mount Jagungal (6,775 feet). It is hard to do justice to the magnificence and grandeur of the last-named mountain. It is a characteristic Australian peak, its crouching-lion form sparkling and blazing from a diamond-studded mantle of snow.

Other peaks of well over 6,000 feet, in this glorious snow country between Kosciusko and Kiandra, include Mount Twynam, Mount Lee, Mount Clarke, Mount Tait, Gill's Knob, Granite Heights and Bull's Peaks. The snow country around Kosciusko itself covers an area of something like 300 square miles. All the way from Charlotte's Pass (Kosciusko) to Kiandra, the exploring skier can travel along the range—a distance of nearly sixty miles—without any danger of running out of snow. Mount Townsend, close to Charlotte's Pass, is a first-class downhill course; 2,500 feet of vertical descent. Townsend's alpine quality is exciting enough to put the top-flight international skier on his mettle. All around this area is a network of glittering valleys. They join the majestic Northcote Canyon, and give the area a name that is strikingly apt— Little Austria. Not far away, and only three miles from the Kosciusko Chalet, is Mount Twynham (7,000 feet), whose western face provides a swift, uninterrupted run that European skiers compare favourably with Kitzbuhl, the famous snow resort in the Austrian Tyrol. There is no doubt that the immense ski-ing fields between Kosciusko and Kiandra are among the finest to be found in the world. It is equally certain that the bulk of this vast plateau is at present absolutely unknown to even the experienced skier. The skiers of today keep to the hotel and chalet areas, with their chair-lifts and tows. They show little or no interest in what lies beyond the peaks.

After the discovery of Mount Kosciusko in 1840 by Strzelecki, other explorers, botanists, geologists and meteorologists studied the area from time to time but, like Strzelecki, only in the summer season. It was not until 1897 that Kosciusko was scaled for the first time in winter. Much confusion has arisen by the various explorers naming and renaming peaks after themselves, their friends, or public officials, so that when consulting early maps one is often in doubt as to which peak is referred to. It seems a pity that the old euphonious Aboriginal names for the various mountains and ranges were not retained.

The first winter ascent of Kosciusko was made by Charles Kerry, who led the party which made the successful climb. Its members comprised fifteen horsemen with five packhorses, and the skis were carried as lances. They set out from Jindabyne, and spent about a week on the journey there and back. The summit was reached at two o'clock on the afternoon of 19 August, 1897.

The majority of Kerry's fifteen were unfamiliar with skis, and no living white man had seen the mountain in its winter garb. All the country above the timber line was a *terra incognita*; and the fact that twelve of the fifteen succeeded in climbing to the top and returning to the camp at Friday Flat in one day is remarkable. The climbers abandoned their skis for the final assault on the summit, which was probably made over the Cootapatamba Saddle, the route at present used by skiers. Charles Kerry tells the story in these words:

'By five o'clock in the late moonlight we were all astir, and daybreak found thirteen of us tracking in Indian file across the open snow and making for the mountain, each man bearing only his skis, with, for divisible ballast, a camera and a tomahawk; and in his pocket some luncheon as his appetite warranted; wisest he who estimated his capacity before his early breakfast.

' "Thirteen of us, and starting from Friday Flat—that sounds bad", growled a superstitious one as we headed for the timber. It did appear ominous, and especially as next morning we found that ski-ing was impracticable by reason of the denseness of the timber, and that there was nothing for it but a bold plunge into the snow, which lay lightly some three feet or more on the top of the thick undergrowth. Ten minutes of this and our leader stopped exhausted. It looked bad, but the second man was pushing on in his place, and thus early it fell that we learned that each must do his five minutes' spell of track breaking in turn, the rest following closely in his footsteps.

'Thus for three hours and a half, with the taciturnity bred of breathlessness and with perspiration pouring out of every pore, we literally struggled upwards, our backward track resembling the path of a miniature snow plough, springing from which bracken and undergrowth raised surprised heads to meet the world weeks before their springtime. Four hours and the snow grew noticeably firmer; another half-hour, and when it seemed that all our day would be exhausted without more result than indefinite struggling, we emerged from the forest into wonderland.

'A great drift, overhanging a huge cave, topped the last of the timber, and when we had scaled its frosty sides, on hands and knees, we pulled up for a breather and waited for a normal heart-beat from that palpitating organ. Also, we were photographed in our last prideful flounder, for did not our aneroid show that we had ascended 1,800 foot, although we had accomplished but two miles of the estimated eight. Ski now, and with a few luxurious rhythmical strides we had gained a point a vantage farther than we could see the night before, and had an open look-out for weather signs.

' "The day of the year!" we shouted in acclamation to a cloudless sky and a vast sunlit snow plain which stretched before us all unbroken by vegetation or granite outcrop. Not destitute of fauna, though far over this trackless expanse ahead of us sped two hares. This proved first-class travelling for skis, and briskly we glided on, all gay, but with a growing thirst, and here the thrice-accursed "snowbias" first overtook us. Before starting each man had solemnly adjured his neighbour not to eat snow. But there was no water and we had by this time learned that snow mixed with whisky instantly went into hard ice at the bottom of our flask cups; thus it came about that, in direst need, the first handful of snow went furtively into the writer's mouth, and therefore he bemoaned his weakness until presently he discovered that everyone else was doing the same. As noon came, and a halt was proclaimed for luncheon, a similar general weakness was disclosed, for when the contents of our pockets should have been produced, it was found they had mysteriously vanished before a much earlier hunger.

'Therefore, on again towards a distant ruggedness which, bordering the tablelands, rose gaunt and desolate, surely a white-palled barrier to all further progress. "Have we to climb that?" cried one of us in dismay. "We had," said our guides, recognising in its broken outline some familiar shape; but, they added, from its summit we should overlook the valley which lay immediately below our ambitious goal. By this time, however, several of us felt that if the view from this eminence disclosed much further distance to cover we should never get there. Already one of our party had cried "A go," and lay temporarily prostrate upon his skis. Anyhow, we would scale this ridge and see the prospect. So at it we went; the intervals between widening as each man with dogged persistence tackled the snow cliff on his own, choosing the route he fancied easiest. Our guides had given us a direction. More they could not do, for they were as tired as we were and not so young.

'In this rarefied atmosphere our breath came thick and fast, our faces felt and looked like leather, an all-consuming thirst made our dried tongues cleave to the drier palate. "A pound for a pint of water," murmured someone in front. The only response was an advanced bid. Half mechanically we at length breasted the wall, and then what a view met our eyes. The guides were probably most astonished, for they had been here before and now did not recognise their summer valley. Here was a steep snow gorge, certainly rolling away from us smoothly; but where, in its depths, should have been Cootapatamba (the highest sheet of water in Australia) and the head waters of the Murray River, the winter coverlet rolled on uninterruptedly, until opposite us it rose again in a sheer wall to a narrow plateau fully a mile in length. Over this plateau hung an enormous drift, roofing it in down its whole length, and supported, as we could just make out, by regular columns and groinings of frozen snow.

'A little to the left of this there rose a marbled peak, to which we took off our hats respectfully, for we knew it instinctively. Its unexpected proximity gave new life to us as we headed for it, but speedy progress we soon found impossible by reason of the frozen glacier-like slopes around the head of the valley. One false step and instant descent to the depths below; indeed, one of our party nearly took that short cut, and only by dint of careful planting of alpen-stock made inch by inch a sober return to us.

'One by one we abandoned our snow-shoes, our feet leaving little impression on the crackling snow, and now for the final pinch. A quarter of a mile to go and five hundred feet. Eventually the summit was reached by twelve of the party at 2 p.m., the first to reach the goal being guide J. Boulton, who thus won the gold medal offered for the first man to reach the summit. The cairn and survey mark were found to be entirely covered with frozen snow which had been blown by the winds into fantastical and stalactitic formations, presenting in the brilliant sunshine a dazzling picture never to be forgotten by the elated explorers . . .'

EIGHTEEN

The First Skiers

IT was in the old New South Wales mining township of Kiandra that Australia's ski-ing began; and here, fittingly enough, that her first ski-ing organization had its birth. Kiandra—Australia's coldest township—lies at the northern end of a seventy-five-mile range. Skis were known generally in Kiandra as 'snow-shoes', and the first club was called a snow-shoe club; while the 'carnivals' were always described as snow-shoe races. The modern term, 'ski', came into use in Kiandra very early in this century.

In about 1860, a Norwegian miner who was a relative of explorer Roald Amundsen, first man to reach the South Pole, was amongst those who settled in this small alpine mining village. He made the first pair of snow-shoes from a couple of palings, turned up at one end, and bound to his boots with a single wide strap. Until then, the miners used to leave Kiandra each winter because the place was snowed-up. It was this same Norwegian who, together with some miners from the Austrian Tyrol, first introduced ski-running to Australia, and made the township habitable in winter. As in its birthplace, Norway, ski-ing in Australia began as a purely utilitarian method of getting about in snow-covered country. But it was not long before the spirit of competition crept in, and ski-ing became a sport as well. The Kiandra skiers formed a club and held races, even in the early 1860s, when the township had a population of nearly 10,000 people.

In his book, *The Story of Ski-ing*, Sir Arnold Lunn, the English author and skier, says that ski-ing in Australia began at a much earlier date: 'Skis were used in Tasmania as far back as the 1830s by the fur hunters.' However, the distinguished author's 'skis' were more probably Canadian-type snow shoes.

The first record of ski-ing at Kiandra was published in *The Sydney Morning Herald* of 6 August, 1861 (being reprinted from *The Monaro Mercury*, published in Cooma). It reads as follows:

'Kiandra is a rather dreary place in the winter, but yet the people are not without their amusements. The heaven-pointing snow-clad mountains afford them some pleasure. Scores of young people are frequently engaged climbing the lofty summits with snow-shoes and then sliding down with a volancy that would do credit to some of our railway trains.'

Another account of Kiandra in the same newspaper states:

'No idea can be formed except from actual experience of the horrors of a winter in that part of the country. The roads are impassable except with snow shoes . . . constructed of two palings turned up at the front, and about four foot long, with straps to put the feet in, and the traveller carries a long stick to balance himself, and to assist him up hill. Down hill they can go as fast as a steamer, and on a level with the aid of the pole they can make good headway.'

Before the introduction of skis or snow shoes, the Kiandra mailman risked his life to keep the town in contact with the outside world. When a man ventured out into the snow he took a mate with him, so that if he floundered into a deep drift there would be someone to pull him out. Many gold diggings were frozen and unworkable; those which could be mined were almost inaccessible. In such conditions, Australian ski-ing was born.

A visitor to Kiandra in those early days told a Sydney newspaper reporter that his journey took him to what was almost the region of eternal snow. 'They have it, at any rate, for about nine months of the year,' he added. He spoke of the beauty of the Kiandra district in winter, and said that the effect of the icicles and snow on the trees and shrubs was enchanting. (Nine-tenths of Australians at that time had never seen snow or ice, and in fact were astonished to learn of the existence of such in their country.)

'How did the inhabitants fare?' the informant was asked.

'Oh, they do well,' he replied. 'The Kiandra people require no pity. They would not change places with anyone in the colony. The only wonder is that more visitors do not come to the district in winter and take part in the ski races. Of course, everything gets frozen,' he warned. 'They keep their fresh meat for five months. When they want any, they saw or chop a block off. The milk is solid and the eggs freeze. In the bar of the hotel everything except the spirits is frozen. I took some ale in ice form as an experiment—it was the first time I ever really chewed a drink.'

It was during a severe winter in those pioneering days that one of Australia's strangest newspapers was published at Kiandra. Heavy snowstorms blocking the roads into the township prevented newsprint reaching the publisher of the weekly newspaper. Not to be beaten, he bought up all the calico from a local store, and printed the newspaper on sheets of calico. The snow continued to fall for several weeks so the publisher sent boys around to the miners' homes to collect the calico sheets from previous issues—as there was no more calico available. These were washed and dried and used for each issue until the road to Cooma was opened, and newsprint could be brought in.

At this time approximately 700 Chinese worked on the Kiandra goldfields. Their quarters were in camps separated from the white diggers, and they lived as a separate community, complete with their Joss House. The Chinese were industrious miners, and well-behaved, never drinking alcohol to excess.

In 1860, when bitter winter conditions prevented packhorse teams getting through to the township, some enterprising residents established the Celestial Transport Company, and engaged 200 Chinese at £2 per week to carry all kinds of goods to and from Kiandra. The goods were slung on long poles, which were stretched across the shoulders; and each Chinese was required daily to carry loads of sixty pound over a distance of about fourteen miles. Some carried much heavier loads, up to a hundred and forty pound. Their reputation spread, and was such that they were often referred to as the 'Camels of Kiandra'.

This unusual transport service was not only of benefit to the out-of-work Chinese, but it also proved invaluable to storekeepers and the settlers generally. And, of course, the Company itself benefited in no small measure. One account reveals that £12 a ton was charged for transporting timber and shingles over the snow country per medium of the Chinese porters. When the printing machinery for the first publication of Kiandra's newspaper, the *Alpine Pioneer*, was snowbound on its way to the township, fifty Chinese were engaged to transport the load to its destination. Four thousand four hundred pounds of printing plant were hauled by hand a distance of fourteen miles over broken, mountainous country heavily covered with snow.

It was the Kiandra country that was chosen for Australia's first organised tour of the snowfields. The wording of the pamphlet, issued by the Director of the New South Wales Tourist Bureau, is worth quoting:

THE SNOW REGIONS OF NEW SOUTH WALES. In order to give the residents of New South Wales an opportunity of enjoying an unique holiday, the Government Tourist Bureau has arranged a Tour of the Snow Regions of the Southern District to take in the Kiandra Ski Carnival, giving tourists six days on the snow-shoes. The tour, as will be seen from the itinerary on the back page, is a comprehensive one, embracing a Railway Journey to Cooma, Coach through Adaminaby to Kiandra, Snow-shoe to Yarrangobilly Caves, Coach to Tumut, thence Rail to Sydney. The Round Trip will occupy ten days (from July 15th to 25th), and the fare of £11 will cover all expenses, including the provision of snow-shoes, first-class accommodation being provided everywhere.

Kiandra is snowed-up, so far as vehicular traffic is concerned, for several months of the year. The coaches will not be able to get nearer than within about six miles of the township, and the visitors must complete the journey on snow-shoes. The members of the Kiandra Snow-shoe Club, of which Mr. C. H. Kerry is the Sydney representative, will, however, meet the party and conduct them into Kiandra, so novices will experience very little difficulty in making the journey.

Naturally, in Kiandra, which is the highest town in Australia, the accommodation is very limited, and therefore the number of tickets issued will be a fixed quantity. To those who have never seen deep snow, and have never dropped down precipitous slopes at sixty miles per hour, this tour proves a veritable revelation . . .

As gold-mining ceased, the town of Kiandra died, until there were very few people actually resident there. Still, with the assistance of the surrounding district and skiers from Sydney, they maintained their club and annual snow sports to the present day. A few reminders of the early pioneering days are still to be seen—deserted and dilapidated buildings, old diggings, and even a dam or two constructed by the miners. The miners used the dams to establish systems of canals called 'races', sometimes several miles long, which conveyed water to points along the gold workings. Here it passed into canvas hoses under pressure, and emerged as jets which were used for cutting away overburden and washing the gold-bearing gravel.

In a small way, the miners did with pick and shovel what modern science is doing on the Snowy Mountains Scheme today. They built the first dams in the area, and created history by harnessing the power of the wasted waters from the snow-capped peaks. The dams that still stand are a tribute to sore muscles, blistered hands and pioneer determination. All are remarkably similar in design to the mighty earth and rock-fill structures which today are taming the mountain streams and rivers. One of the miners' dams, three miles from Kiandra, is still holding back 436 million gallons of water. This is the Three Mile Dam. It is 45 feet high, 500 feet long, and 14 feet wide on top.

Today, Kiandra is a very small settlement. Unlike most other ski-ing centres in the Australian snowfields, it is a village where people live and work all through the year.

Kiandra is pleasant country. The hills of snow gums, the plateau, the Eucumbene River chattering a cheerful song, and the slopes of Township Hill constitute a charming scene. The village is especially picturesque on an early frosty morning, with the sun shining out of a limpid blue. After heavy snowfalls, thickly snow-covered trees and shrubs recall alpine scenes in Europe. Wildlife is plentiful in the district, where foxes, wombats and echidna find shelter in the surrounding hills.

NINETEEN

The Strzelecki Story

'HERE is a flower from Mount Kosciusko—the highest peak in Australia—the first in the New World bearing a Polish name. I believe that you will be the first Polish woman to have a flower from that mountain. Let it remind you ever of freedom, patriotism and love . . .' So wrote Paul Edmund de Strzelecki to his boyhood sweetheart when he returned to Sydney in 1840, after climbing the Australian Alps, and naming the highest peak he found after the Polish hero, Kosciusko.

'The particular configuration of this eminence,' he recorded, 'struck me so forcibly by the similarity it bears to a tumulus elevated in Krakow over the tomb of the patriot Kosciusko that, although in a foreign country, on foreign ground, but amongst a free people who appreciate freedom and its votaries, I could not refrain from giving it the name of Mount Kosciusko.'

Paul Edmund de Strzelecki, a Pole by birth, became a naturalized Englishman, a Knight Commander of the Bath, and a Knight Commander of St. Michael and St. George. He ran away from home—a country house in Prussian Poland—and, without help of family, won a distinguished position in England during the Victorian era. Although given the title 'Count' by many of his contemporaries, particularly in Australia, Strzelecki was not a count. He was a Polish nobleman, or *szlachcic*. The word is difficult to translate; there is no exact equivalent in the British system of graduation of nobility. In Poland, apart from Princes—mostly of Royal descent—there was only one class of nobility. In some regards,

134

the privileges of Polish *szlachta*, or noblemen, were no lower than those of the high nobility of Western Europe.

Contrary to the statements of some modern writers, there is no evidence that Paul Strzelecki ever signed or introduced himself as a 'count'. In 1834, on the passenger list of the ship *Virginian*, he wrote simply, 'gentleman'; and in 1845, on his naturalization papers, he described himself as 'Monsieur'. Then, in 1873, in a letter to Maria Reidt, he stated plainly: 'only for courtesy reason Lord Colchester adorned my name with the title of count.' Many examples can be found of members of the Polish *szlachta* being addressed as counts when abroad.

Paul Strzelecki spent in Australia only five years (1839–1843); but during that time he made history. Strzelecki was chiefly interested in the mineralogy and geology of Australia, and was one of the first discoverers of her gold, and of Tasmania's first coal. Travelling on foot over 7,000 miles of New South Wales, Victoria, and Tasmania, he made the first extensive geological and mineralogical survey of the regions he crossed. He was the first to survey and delineate the present Australian Capital Territory; he discovered and named Gippsland and its Snowy River, charted the coast of Victoria from Wilson's Promontory to Sealers' Cove, and explored the Bass Strait Islands.

In 1839 Strzelecki located traces of gold both in pyrites near Hartley and in quartz near Wellington, New South Wales. Governor Gipps feared, however, that an announcement of such a discovery would make it impossible to maintain discipline in the penal colony, and he persuaded Strzelecki (as others before him had been persuaded) to keep it secret. He did so to the extent that in his journal, published in the *Sydney Herald* of 19 August, 1841, he spoke of gold having been found, 'sufficient to attest its presence; insufficient to repay its extraction'. He had, however, reason to think that gold in larger quantities could be found in the Bathurst district, but respected the Governor's wishes in saying nothing further.

Not until James Macarthur revealed the facts in the Legislative Council of New South Wales in 1853 was it generally known that Strzelecki was the first successful gold-digger in Australia. (In demonstrating the priority of

Strzelecki's claim over that of Hargraves, in discovering gold in the Bathurst-Wellington district, Macarthur overlooked a find made sixteen years before Strzelecki's examination of the Western district. On 15 February, 1823, James McBrien found gold in the hills along the Fish River between Rydal and Bathurst.)

Strzelecki was born in June, 1797, in the Polish province of Poznan. This had been seized only three years before by Prussia when, in spite of the heroism of the great Polish patriot, Kosciusko, Poland fell under the blows of the German and Russian armies. At the age of fourteen, he was sent by his father to a school in Warsaw, and lodged at the home of his father's friend. Two years later he went home, and in the absence of his parents packed his bags and disappeared for five years. He enlisted as a soldier during this period and on his return home fell in love with a girl of fifteen, Adyna Turno. She loved him in return; but she was the daughter of a wealthy family, and her father did not approve of the match.

The young couple met in secret and planned an elopement, but Adyna's father discovered the plot and made things so uncomfortable for Paul that he left home, never to return. But Adyna did not forget him; she remained his sweetheart, and died unmarried. Paul became a student at the Heidelberg University, and in 1830 travelled to Scotland, where he did post-graduate work in science, and explored the northern Highlands. Four years later he went to North and South America, and then set out for Australia.

After discovering and naming Mount Kosciusko, Strzelecki entered Victoria and named the region he passed through, 'Gippsland', after his friend, Governor Gipps. He worked backwards and forwards in the region of the Snowy River, and then moved south for further exploration. Later, in 1840, he set out for Tasmania, where Sir John Franklin, the famous Arctic explorer, was Governor. Franklin welcomed Strzelecki, and placed every official assistance at his disposal. The matter of Strzelecki's observations came to be the basis of Launceston's water supply, and of the great irrigation scheme now harnessing the mighty waters of the island's lakes—the hydro-electric

The old Berrima (N.S.W.) Gaol entrance (page 102)

Trail-riding in the Great Divide (pages 91, 92)

undertaking whose ultimate potential is estimated at more than three million horsepower.

In 1842, still assisted by Governor Franklin, Strzelecki explored the islands of Bass Strait, Wilson's Promontory, Sealers' Cove and Corner Inlet. The following year he returned to England, and was gratified to receive an address from the Tasmanian public, accompanied by the sum of £400, in recognition of his geological work. His published scientific work, *Physical Description of New South Wales and Van Diemen's Land* (Victoria then being included in the colony of New South Wales), was for many years a standard textbook on the subject.

The Royal Geographical Society honoured the author with its gold medal; and Strzelecki applied for and was granted British naturalization. Later he was honoured with the degree, honorary Doctor of Civil Law, at Oxford; and the Order of St. Michael and St. George was conferred on him for his Australian discoveries. He gave his attention to philanthropic interests, and especially to assisting the emigration of impoverished families to Australia. In this he was associated with Caroline Chisholm—'the greatest of Australia's women pioneers'. He died in 1873, at his London house in Saville Row, having reached the age of seventy-seven.

Strzelecki's name is commemorated in a number of places in Australia: these are a range in southern Victoria; a creek in north-eastern South Australia; a township in Victoria, south of Warragul; a peak on Flinders Island, Bass Strait; and a mountain in the Northern Territory, about 170 miles north of Alice Springs. The Strzelecki Ranges, in the mountainous country to the north and north-east of Korumburra, in western Gippsland, was originally heavily forested and inaccessible, but most of it has been cleared, principally for dairying, for which it is considered one of the finest areas in Victoria.

In October 1967, Polish people from Queensland, and metropolitan and country areas of New South Wales, Victoria and South Australia, joined a ceremony in the Perisher Valley of the Kosciusko region. This was to commemorate the 150th anniversary of the death of General Tadeusz Kosciusko (the Polish spelling is Kosciuszko). The ceremony began with a Mass

Australian snowfields are lower than most of those in other countries, but they are in many ways superior and safer
(page 120)

conducted by Fr. Warzecha of Canberra, at the Perisher Church, and there was a Polish choir from Canberra and Queanbeyan. The ex-Polish Army Chaplain led the congregation in a Unitarian prayer for the souls of Kosciusko, and of Strzelecki and other explorers. At the same time, a former Polish Air Force and R.A.F. fighter pilot dropped flowers on the summit of Mount Kosciusko.

General Tadeusz Kosciuszko, the famed Polish freedom fighter, never married; but eighty-one people in Australia are direct descendants of his family. Fifty of these attended the ceremony, the ski races, and the glittering ball that followed. A fifth generation of the family is now appearing in Australia, all tracing their descent from the General's brother.

'Kosciuszko, look at us from Heaven!' sang the Polish troops, when charging enemy lines. His name in Poland is revered and worshipped no less—and perhaps more—than that of a saint. It is estimated that about 1,200 poems have been written about him, and as many books, pamphlets, plays and musical compositions. His picture, in which he appears clad in the white mantle of a Cracovian peasant, hangs in thousands of homes throughout the country. Every Polish child knows his name, and every high school student knows the story of his life—his victories, his failures, and his indomitable struggle for freedom and equality for all.

Kosciuszko was born in Poland on 12 February, 1746, and brought up in the liberal atmosphere of hopes and aspirations for social changes prevailing in Poland at the time. He fervently believed in freedom of the individual, self-determination of nations, equality in front of the law, equality of opportunity and classless society. He was one of the early protagonists of social changes; one of the many whose great struggle resulted in the modern social structure enjoyed by us today.

Kosciuszko chose an army career and, after completing his studies as an artillery and fortifications officer, served for a time. Soon, however, he heard that Washington was raising the flag of freedom and independence in America; he went there and offered his services. It has been told that when Washington looked up from papers Kosciuszko presented to him and asked what he could do, Kosciuszko answered quietly: 'Try me and see.'

Kosciuszko rose to the rank of Brigadier-General of American Armies fighting for independence, and earned a land grant and a substantial pension. He returned to Poland, however, to lead his people in the struggle for freedom and self-determination. He led an army of peasants—the first time peasants had banded together for battle—and prayed with them before the Battle of Raclawice, in which they defeated the Russians.

Later the Russians were joined by Prussian and Austrian forces to overrun the Polish forces. Kosciuszko was wounded, taken prisoner, and spent two years in a Russian gaol. He went to America after his release, but the call of his homeland was too strong; and after a few months he returned again to Poland during the Napoleonic period, and continued his work for his country's freedom. He died quietly on 15 October, 1817.

TWENTY

Thredbo and the Perisher Valley

LOCATED in the Thredbo Valley of the Kosciusko State Park is an alpine holiday resort of international standard. The Thredbo village is a complete unit. There are chalets, lodges, shops, a medical centre, service station, and bank; and a ski kindergarten, for the benefit of parents with young children. Dominating the village is the Thredbo Alpine Hotel with its viewing tower, shop arcade, skating rink and private terraces. One of its dining areas seats 150 people, and there are cocktail bars and night clubs, together with a resident band and guest artists.

The Snowy Mountains rise two thousand feet above the village, built on the side of the valley beneath. Nearly three miles of chair-lifts take skiers into the deep snow up top, where they have a choice of fifteen ski trails to the bottom station. Chairlifts and T-bars can transport about 2,800 skiers an hour—the chairlift to the top of Mount Crackenback (6,350 feet) takes fifteen minutes. Because of this difference in altitude between the village and Mount Crackenback, the former is protected; the snow never lies on the ground more than three or four feet deep in Thredbo village, and the road to it is kept open all winter.

The name Crackenback is derived from a 'pidgin English' word—'Crack-em-back'. Some Aborigines with a smattering of English who camped in that area referred to the steepness of the range by saying that the ascent of it would crack a man's back—'crack-em-back'. The Crackenback Peak rises above the Thredbo River in a horizontal distance of one and a quarter miles. Behind Crackenback the slopes of the Ramshead Range rise to over 7,000 feet, making a total ascent of 2,600 feet in two-and-a-half miles from the village site. Crackenback Peak is only two-and-three-quarter miles from the summit of Mount Kosciusko. The slopes of Crackenback include every variety of gradient, and because of their southerly aspect, and proximity to the top of the Main Dividing Range, they have an unusually long snow season.

The Alpine Way linking Jindabyne and Khancoban in the Upper Murray district, has made the Thredbo village area easily accessible to visitors from other States. The Alpine Way travels up the Thredbo Valley from Jindabyne until it crosses the Great Dividing Range at Dead Horse Gap, twenty-six miles from Jindabyne; and from there it descends to the Murray River, at Tom Groggin Camp. The latter, oddly enough, was not a man's name, but is in fact the white man's corruption of the Aboriginal word, 'ton-a-roggin', which is what the natives called a species of water spider prevalent in the area. Dead Horse Gap, in the same area, was named by stockmen, presumably because one of their horses died there.

Another tremendously popular ski-ing resort in the New South Wales region of the Australian Alps is the beautiful Perisher Valley. It, too, has its luxury hotels, chalets, and lodges—even a supermarket with a snowmobile delivery service—and a ski school staffed by some of the world's leading instructors from overseas. In mid-winter the road to the Perisher Valley is not open beyond Smiggin Holes, so from here one must travel by snowmobile.

What is now Smiggin Holes was originally known by the stockmen using it as a staging camp as 'The Licks', because it was one of the places at which they put out blocks of salt-lick for their cattle. A young Scottish migrant was sent with stores for the camp, and after looking around asked why they called it 'The Licks'. Told the reason, the young Scot, conscious of his ancestry, said 'It's not "The Licks" you should call it. In Scotland where I come from, and where salt-licks are so placed for cattle, the animals in licking the salt make holes in the ground which we call "Smiggin Holes".' And Smiggin Holes it has been ever since.

The Perisher area, in the days of the early snow leases, was an important place for stockmen. From Perisher one trail led over Perisher Gap to the Kosciusko region, and further trails branched off to the Snowy River and to the grass flats near Pounds Creek, and to Mount Twynam. One story suggests that the Perisher was so-named because some cattle were caught there by the first winter snows, and perished. The more likely version attributes the naming to a well-known pioneer, Jimmy Spencer, after whom Spencer's Creek in the vicinity is named. It seems that one early winter Jimmy and his stockmen were rounding up cattle in the area before they were trapped by the first heavy snows. They travelled up through Perisher Gap and on reaching a crest were met by a sudden cold gust of wind which almost swept them off their feet. Jimmy turned to a companion and is reputed to have said, 'My God, this is a perisher!'

It was whilst crossing the creek now bearing his name that Jimmy Spencer had the misfortune to fall in it one day. His fellow stockmen catching sight of Spencer's head and big beard in the cold stream said facetiously: 'If he wants to have a swim he can have it to himself.' So they called it Spencer's Creek. Piper's Gap and Piper's Creek also owe their names to the activities of Jimmy Spencer. Piper was in fact a particularly powerful and fractious lead bullock in Spencer's team, which always broke loose at night on trips to the area, and was usually found feeding next morning at the spot now known as Piper's Gap.

Thredbo, Perisher Valley, and other snow resorts in the area, are included in the Kosciusko State Park, which covers some 2,100 square miles. The mountains and gorges of the park—the largest in Australia—stretch for more than 100 miles north from the New South Wales-Victorian border, and its average width is 25 miles. In 1944 the New South Wales Government decided to establish the park to preserve its wild beauty. Hunting or trapping of birds, animals and insects is prohibited.

Firearms are outlawed, and it is illegal to pick wild-flowers or remove plant or rock specimens. About 100 square miles, surrounding the summit of Mount Kosciusko, have been declared a primitive area, the first of its kind in Australia.

Here some of nature's rarest marsupials live in undisturbed peace. There is the great grey (or grey forester) kangaroo, one of the world's largest marsupials; the brush-tailed rock wallaby; glider and ringtail possums; the echidna; the wombat; and the platypus. The echidna, or spiny-anteater, and the platypus, are the two oldest and most primitive of mammals; and the only two furred animals in the world that lay eggs. Although the young are nourished with milk from the mother, neither the platypus nor the echidna has teats. Both lay eggs with a leathery shell that is compressible, not brittle like birds' eggs. Both, too, are grouped in a sub-class of their own, the *Monotremata*, referring to the fact that each animal has one single orifice for excretion and for reproduction, like the birds and reptiles.

The platypus is partly aquatic and lives where there is permanent water. Mostly it hides in a burrow during the day and spends part of the night hunting in the water, and sometimes eating larger prey, such as yabbies, on land. An adult platypus is about two feet long, usually dark brown dorsally and orange red, or yellowish brown ventrally, with a tail like that of a beaver. It has a conspicuous and characteristic duckbill, a highly developed sensory organ adapted for foraging under the water. The sensory nerves on the soft leathery duckbill guide the platypus to food (it always swims with eyes and ears closed), and this it carries alive to the surface. A versatile feeder, the animal takes almost any kind of aquatic insect, and tackles crustaceans, as well as worms, grubs, and similar small fry. The feet of the platypus are webbed, and the legs extremely short. The female breeds in a burrow where males are not allowed. She makes a rough nest of leaves and bark, and generally lays two eggs. The young are about half-an-inch long, and remain attached to the mother's skin for a few days; rubbing her chest stimulates a milk-flow through enlarged pores to nourish the young.

All animals have some defensive mechanism, and the

platypus and the echidna are no exceptions. In spite of their primitiveness, each can take good care of itself. The male platypus, for instance, has a spur on the back of each hind leg, connected to a poison sac; a wound from this spur can be quite painful. The echidna, on the other hand, has an armour of quills, and an ability to dig itself into the ground rapidly, so that it presents only its spiny back—offering nothing to grasp and no undefended points to attack.

The echidna is an ant-eater, with a tube-like bill, which cannot be opened as birds open their bills. Through a hole in the bill, the echidna's enormously long and sticky tongue is protruded to catch ants. The mammal's eyesight is poor, but the sense of smell is an adequate substitute. Its body is covered with quills and its claws, particularly the hind ones, are huge. The female develops a rudimentary pouch during the breeding season, and in it the egg, or perhaps two eggs, are placed. Echidnas do not make burrows but hide under logs, under bushes, or in the abandoned burrows of other animals. They are very powerful creatures, and by shoving and pushing will remove rocks about their own size to uncover a nest of ants underneath.

Like these and other strange animals found nowhere else in the world, the wombat is as much a part of Australia as the gum trees, and is among the living antiques. The wombat is a grass-feeder and a burrow-digger. Indeed, its burrow can be a fantastic excavation, sometimes a hundred feet long and several feet in diameter. A powerful animal, weighing up to eighty pound, the wombat is compactly built, barrel-shaped, with a flat stocky head and short but very thick and hard-muscled legs. It cannot run quickly, but moves fast in dense bush, its low tough body and flat head pushing through the undergrowth. The female bears one, or at most two, young ones a year, and carries its babies in its pouch for a long time.

Wombats are so unlike other marsupials that, to classify them, a special zoological family had to be created. Strangely enough, they are related to the arboreal possums and koalas, although totally unlike physically and in habits; they look more like tailless beavers. Their teeth are rootless, and grow continuously, to offset normal wear. All wombats would seem to be fairly gregarious, and small colonies of these curious creatures live more or less together in the same piece of bush. They emerge from their burrows in the late afternoon and spend the evening and the night moving about—feeding, huffing, and growling—as they tear up the soil in characteristic digging activities.

Birdlife, too, in the Kosciusko State Park, is rich in variety and colour. Parrots and cockatoos include the crimson rosella, the gang-gang cockatoo, the yellow-tailed black cockatoo and the white cockatoo. The latter is a raucous member of the noisy parrot family, more numerous in Australia than in any other country. There are five kinds of black cockatoos with different colour patches on their tails. The red-banded tail feathers were favourite ornaments for the Aborigines' headdresses, and ceremonial objects used in their corroborees.

The cockatoo is an intelligent and wary bird. When the birds are feeding (often damaging crops), sentinels are usually posted in neighbouring trees to give warning of the approach of danger. This has given rise to the Australian slang term, 'cockatoo', for a sentinel who is posted outside an illicit gambling centre.

With the coming of spring, the snow retreats above the lower slopes; and in its place an army of snow daisies rises to take possession of the alps, covering them with millions of blooms. It seems a miracle that these sturdy mountaineers should survive the long winter, snowbound; and yet far more delicate little plants welcome the spring on the roof of Australia. Here you may see an astonishing variety of wildflowers—black-eyed buttercups, violets, ranunculi, bluebells, alpine orchids. The higher altitudes are the home of an arresting alpine heath, with many rigid spikes of pale creamy-yellow flowers. Pimelias abound lower down, and around the granite rocks flourish a richly fragrant mint-bush and innumerable gaily coloured miniatures. Everywhere else the entire slopes are covered with myriads of silvery-leafed snow daisies.

TWENTY-ONE

The Victorian Alps

THE Australian Alps extend from the Kosciusko area into north-eastern Victoria, where the snowfields extend to within sixty miles of Melbourne. As in New South Wales, the Victorian Alps have been smoothed by millions of years of erosion; so that the peaks, many of which are over 6,000 feet in height, have gentle slopes, idyllically free of the hazards of avalanches, precipices, or glaciers. Victoria has more ski clubs than New South Wales—perhaps because its capital, unlike Sydney, is in the fortunate position of having good ski-ing grounds so close to the city—and its peaks at Hotham, Buller, the glorious Bogong Mountain, and Mount Feathertop, have everything for the skilled racer, who likes to feel the cut of the wind as he runs the steepest *schuss* straight.

Mount Feathertop has been called the Queen of the Alps, and it well deserves that proud title. Feathertop reveals a feminine fickleness in two highly contrasting aspects. Viewed from the north-west she appears smooth and sophisticated, bland yet imperious. From the south-west her mood is seen to have changed with dramatic suddenness. Rugged and steep, Mount Feathertop, heavily arrayed in deep snow, rises abruptly from the surrounding range, and rears herself above the rounded summits of her rivals. To see the serrated, towering peaks of this masterpiece of alpine sculpture piercing an aquamarine sky is a spell-binding experience.

The beautiful Swindlers' Valley nestles close by Mount Hotham, (6,200 feet), a peak of sheer grandeur, in the heart of the Victorian Alps. It offers ski-ing slopes of infinite variety in

146

a setting of majestic scenery featuring Mount Feathertop with its mighty fluted spear-tip ascending to 6,306 feet. Ski touring is a feature of the valleys in the Hotham Heights area. The hosts of slopes, more than one can experience in a single holiday, beckon the skier on all-day outings.

Sheltered from winter's storms, the many ski runs of the popular Mount Higginbotham area of this vast valley are linked at their foot by a trail along the snow-covered water race. A relic of bygone mining days, this leads through a fairyland of snow gums to Begg's Bath, near the take-off on the Blue Ribbon Tow. The latter is perhaps the best on Australia's snowfields, for the number and variety of long ski runs immediately around it. One of these—the 'Varsity Drag'—is a wooded, winding trail sheering fantastically between distorted snow gums.

As in New South Wales, the first white men on these mountains identified landmarks with incidents which had happened there; hence, some of the colourful and unorthodox names. Swindlers' Valley and Swindlers' Creek were so named from a now-forgotten shady deal in the gold-mining days of Hotham. A well-known point on Mount Hotham—'The Gallows'—is called after an old cattle-slaughtering spot. This is the starting point for a ski run called Hangman's Drop. A depression between two ridges at Falls Creek is known as 'the Valley of the Moon'. Oddly shaped cornices jutting from it give the appearance of an eerie moonscape.

Highest peak in the Victorian Alps is dome-topped Mount Bogong (6,506 feet), which provides some of the best ski runs in Australia. The word Bogong is an Aboriginal one and refers to the Bogong moth, an insect which appears in great numbers in springtime. The Bogong is a large brown variety with circles on its wings. Records left by an early squatter named Mansfield, who is honoured in the Victorian town of that name, mention that in certain drought seasons the local Aborigines were sometimes brought to the verge of starvation through lack of food. He states that they then migrated to the mountain regions, and would reappear after several months, sleek and fat. He asked what they did to produce such a transformation, but all they said as they rubbed their stomachs was 'Bogong Bogong'.

Being of an inquiring turn of mind, he determined to go with them one year; and it is interesting to read his description. The whole tribe migrated to the vicinity of the mountain peak, and immediately upon arrival, the gins collected the long, tough grass fibres and made small baskets. The men armed themselves with long sticks, and raked between the rocks for the big fat moths, which abound in this region. They were placed in the baskets made by the women, cooked slowly over the fire, and eaten. This was the source of the natives' well-nourished condition.

Stretching for 280 square miles, deep with snow, the Bogong High Plains lie about 80 miles due south of the New South Wales-Victorian border city of Albury. The road between Albury and the Bogong High Plains passes through Kiewa Valley, a rich dairying country reaching up to the wooded hills. The Kiewa River, which has its source in the snowfields, irrigates the whole fertile valley, and provides some of the best trout fishing in Australia. Running parallel to the Kiewa Valley is the Ovens River Valley, which is equally beautiful. The Victorian Forestry Department has planted thousands of acres of pine forests which cover the hillside for miles on end.

The High Plains, on the Victorian side of the border, have a splendid access road; while visitors from New South Wales may travel to Albury and change to a motor coach which takes them to the snow-line. There are also various plane services that enable even those who live in the tropic north to go ski-ing on the Bogong High Plains in a matter of hours.

Falls Creek, on the edge of the Bogong High Plains, has developed into the second largest of Victoria's alpine villages. One of its many chalets and lodges accommodates 144 guests. Falls Creek has a charm all its own; a charm it owes in part to the fact that it is within the State Electricity Commission territory, so that at night the village twinkles on its mountain-top like something out of a fairytale. Ski-ing history was made at Falls Creek on 21 July, 1957, when the first passengers were carried on the first Alpine Chair Lift to operate on Australia's snowfields.

Victoria's oldest-established snow resort, Mount Buffalo, is considered a little genteel and unexciting by the thrill-seeking skiers. The great hump of 'Buffalo', its four thousand feet dominating the north-eastern Victorian landscape, is so varied and beautiful in its scenery that it has never been a purely seasonal resort. Waterfalls, gorges, a lake, great delicately-balanced granite formations, a spring carpet of wildflowers—these are the magnets that attract visitors to Buffalo all the year round.

The peak is part of a spectacular series of granite mountains, which at their highest point rise to 5,645 feet above sea-level. The name was bestowed by the explorers Hume and Hovell on 25 November, 1824; they state in their journal that they saw on that day, 'a mountain with snow upon it . . . a singular-looking mountain which we called Mount Buffalo'.

From north to south, the range is seven miles long; and from east to west, about four miles across at its widest part. A deep valley, in which Buffalo Creek flows, divides North Buffalo from the Buffalo proper. In general, the surface of the plateau some thirteen-and-a-half square miles—is remarkable for the abundance of the tors and granite blocks that are strewn over it; but between the rocky hills are narrow plains that are bare of trees, and free from granite blocks. The Gorge, a wall of granite up to 800 feet high, and half a mile long, is a striking feature. Other natural features of the area are extraordinarily balanced boulders known as Egg Rock, The Sentinel, and The Cathedral.

The Cathedral is a slab-sided, five-hundred-foot-high mass of granite rising from the heart of the plateau. The way to the summit, where a man-made cross complements nature's architecture, leads first along winding, gently sloping bush paths; then up, over, or around a variety of obstacles that dare many who are there for the first time to test their skill and nerve as rock-climbers. To an experienced climber, The Cathedral poses no great hazards; but those who struggle panting to the few square feet of almost level rock around the cross find in the ascent something of high adventure. However, since the 1930s, many hundreds of them have qualified to sign the book recording all who have climbed The Cathedral, thanks to a veteran guide, Bill Marriott.

The vegetation of the area is mainly open forest; more sparse at higher altitudes. Fauna is not abundant, but it includes the superb lyrebird (*Menura superba*), Buffalo being one of the most distant points from the coast where the species occurs. When a road was constructed up the range, and a governmental chalet built on the plateau, Mount Buffalo became—and remains—one of Australia's most popular resorts, favoured alike for its summer attractions and its winter beauty.

Mount Baw Baw, Donna Buang and Buller are other popular Victorian snow resorts. Mount Buller Alpine Village, 150 miles from Melbourne, is a splendid ski-ing ground for racing preparations, and is often used for national championships. The mountain has ski slopes on three sides, so that it always has at least one face turned to the sun or sheltered from the wind. Chalets and privately-owned lodges at Buller provide accommodation for over 800 people, and more buildings go up every summer. At least one of the lodges is entirely European in character and cuisine. The beds have great feather coverlets that belong typically to European village living.

Nearest town to Mount Buller ski resort is Mansfield, just 20 miles away. It is associated with the Kelly gang, who in 1878 killed three policemen in the Wombat Ranges nearby. A memorial to the three men stands in the town; and the folk-ballad, 'Stringybark Creek', recalls those lawless days:

A sergeant and three constables set out from Mansfield town
Near the end of last October for to hunt the Kellys down;
They started for the Wombat Hills and thought it quite a lark
When they camped upon the borders of a creek called
    Stringybark.

They had grub and ammunition there to last them many a
    week,
And next morning two of them rode out, all to explore the
    creek,
Leaving McIntyre behind them at the camp to cook the grub
And Lonergan to sweep the floor and boss the washing tub.

It was shortly after breakfast Mac thought he heard a noise
So gun in hand he sallied out to try and find the cause,
But he never saw the Kellys planted safe behind a log
So he sauntered back to smoke and yarn and wire into the prog.

But Ned Kelly and his comrades thought they'd like a nearer
  look,
For being short of grub they wished to interview the cook;
And of firearms and cartridges they found they had too few,
So they longed to grab the pistols and the ammunition too.

Both the troopers at a stump alone they were well pleased to see
Watching as the billies boiled to make their pints of tea;
There they joked and chatted gaily never thinking of alarms
Till they heard the fearful cry behind, 'Bail up, throw up your
  arms!'

The traps they started wildly and Mac then firmly stood
While Lonergan made tracks to try and gain the wood,
Reaching round for his revolver but, before he touched the
  stock
Ned Kelly pulled the trigger, fired, and dropped him like a log.

Then after searching McIntyre all through the camp they went
And cleared the guns and cartridges and pistols from the tent,
But brave Kelly muttered sadly as he loaded up his gun,
"Oh, what a bloody pity that the bugger tried to run"

The ballad tells only of the death of Constable Lonigan: the
name is misspelt by the anonymous writer. When the two other
policemen returned to the camp at sunset, the bushrangers
called on them to surrender. They refused and, drawing their
guns, began firing. In the exchanges, 'brave Kelly' shot them
both dead. The three policemen were all Irishmen.

Ski-ing can be thoroughly enjoyed both by the non-expert,
and equally by those whose youthful sporting days are long past.
There is little physical strain involved for those who are content
to ski at their own pace. Within a week, after a few lessons, the
novice can enjoy the thrill of covering the ground in seven-
league boots. You don't want to ski?—you can still enjoy the
alpine scenery, if you have an eye and an ear for beauty. To
sit in a warm room, looking out at the shining white expanse; to
watch great flakes drifting or swirling; to listen to the gentle
rustle of the falling snow: this is one of the most beautiful
things in the world. Snow has a subtle and irresistible charm.
Its jewel-like sprinkling on tree and shrub, fences and roofs,

transforms the most commonplace object into something entrancing.

When summer halts the snow games in the alpine mountains, trout fishing takes over as a holiday magnet. And trout fishing in Australia has reached record proportions; one dedicated troutman recently flew from Scotland for a few days fishing in the Snowy. He was no exception; for tourists from all parts of the world come to try their skill with the big rainbow trout.

Lake Eucumbene, where the trout numbers are believed to exceed Australia's population, has a hundred rivers and streams near the many resort areas, seeded with millions of trout. These have thrived. On Lake Eucumbene, the trout season is open all the year round. In rivers and streams, it is closed from about 30 April to the first week-end in September; to allow the trout to breed. For bait, trout fishermen can legally use insects, worms, minnows, or any artificial lures or spinners.

The Australian trout record is thirty-nine pound; and ten pounders are common. It probably is the most challenging and satisfying type of fishing available; the trout is cunning, and he fights with incredible fury in these snow-fed streams and lakes. Many trout fishermen are interested solely in the sport, not the frying-pan rewards. They use unbarbed hooks, cotton-strength lines, and home-made lures. They believe that the worthy trout earns his freedom, and they put him back in the waters. But it's a rare individual who can resist the thought of delicious fried mountain trout.

The Australian Alps are the home of a songless cicada—the only silent cicada in the world—and a grasshopper which changes its colour according to the weather. The former is a relic of the period before the cicadas acquired their sounding apparatus; and is as far removed from the rest of the family as the Neanderthal man is from human-kind today. Its unique survival may be explained by the loneliness of its snow country habitat, its lack of song, and its nocturnal habits. The cicada-killing wasp does not range into the snow-clad forests of these high altitudes; its silence does not attract birds, while its habit

The Snowy River provides some of the best trout fishing in Australia   (page 152)

Happy evenings in a ski lodge, with voices joined in singing anything from carols to current pop tunes (page 140)

Early view of Victorian mineral springs. Hepburn was originally called Spring Creek, because of

of hiding during the day beneath the loose bark is a further protection.

The Australian Alpine grasshopper's colour change is believed to be Nature's device to help the insect fight the mountain cold. Turning black at night, it is the right colour to absorb heat in the morning, because black is the quickest and best absorber of heat. Out in the summer mountain heat, the grasshopper turns blue, because that colour prevents absorption of the fierce ultraviolet and blue rays of sunlight. In this protection against heat and cold, the colour changes of the insect are automatic.

Another oddity which may be seen in these parts is the spinning gum (*Eucalyptus perriniana*). Found in the alpine areas of Victoria and the snow regions of Tasmania, it has leaves which tend to become loose from the branch. The hole in the centre is still pierced by the branch, however; and drying gives these circular leaves a propeller-like twist, so that the breeze spins them around the branch with a loud whistling sound.

TWENTY-TWO

Gippsland Gold

BETWEEN the Great Dividing Range and the Victorian coast, and extending from the New South Wales border to approximately a line from the town of Dandenong to the western shore of Westernport, lies the fertile country of Gippsland. This rich region of some 12,000 square miles embraces alpine areas, pastoral and agricultural lands, the principal coal deposits of Victoria, and the largest natural lakes and river system in Australia.

Omeo, 'the capital of the Alps', is reached by the scenically superb Omeo Highway; and in the search for gold in the early 1850s this was one of the principal fields. The first strike was made in 1852; a small quantity of gold is still mined at Omeo. McMillan's Lookout on the Omeo-Corryong Road reveals a sweeping panorama of Australia's mountain giants—Hotham, Feathertop, Bogong, and Kosciusko. Here, too, the highest through road in Australia crosses the Victorian Alps at a height of 5,086 feet. Other highlights of Omeo are the Victoria Falls and Cobungra Station, famous for its pedigreed Herefords and the largest cattle station in Victoria.

Bairnsdale, 'The City of the Lakes', is the shopping and business centre of East Gippsland. The Aborigines called it Wy-yung. Bairnsdale was the name of a homestead in the district, so called, it is said, because bairns arrived annually with unfailing regularity. True or false, Bairnsdale is a pleasant place, within easy distance of The Lakes and Glenaladale National Parks; Buchan Caves; and old gold rush towns.

Locked in the innermost recesses of the Baw Baw Ranges in North Gippsland is the gold ghost town of Walhalla, which in its time produced nearly a hundred tons of gold, worth $24 million—an amount which would be more than double that value today. The Walhalla mines—the richest gold mines in Gippsland—were not discovered until the early 1860s, but production continued for half a century. Ned Stringer made the strike that made the town; other strikes in the district had prospectors working every creek; every river and gully. Some believed (according to stories told by the people who still live there) that the name Stringer was an alias, and that he was a former convict from Tasmania. At any rate, many claims were pegged almost immediately, and the town of Stringer's Creek was born, later to be re-named, Walhalla.

The miners came by horseback then, over narrow trails that were later widened to accommodate carts, and then waggons and horse-drawn supply trains going in—and the gold escorts going out. Scarlet-painted coaches, escorted by mounted armed guards, regularly took the gold to Melbourne. The individual prospectors didn't strike it rich, for the mountains protected their treasure well. The real and continuous wealth was in the auriferous quartz, deep within the bowels of the mountains that banked Stringer's Creek. To take it out, equipment, men and money were required. And so the mountains relinquished their treasure to company investors.

At its peak, Walhalla had about a thousand buildings, with forty stores and four churches. The town published two newspapers; and beer made by one of Walhalla's two breweries, using the clear mountain water, was a prize-winner in a Paris exhibition. Today a few houses perched precariously on those hills remain to remind the visitor of the town that used to be. Walhalla had to be built almost perpendicular; and steep trails led to its six suburbs—Mormon Town, Maiden Town, Happy-Go-Lucky, Black Diamond, Holmdale, and West Walhalla—all stretching up, around and through the now forest-covered mountains.

Dreaming of the past, and the forty-odd lonely inhabitants still hoping for a future in gold, the rays of the sun stream through the crimson tips of renewing growths of eucalypts, to fall on a desolate, yet strangely beautiful scene. The chimney of a one-time bank, a well or two, the remains of buildings—mute witnesses of the former glory of Walhalla, once Victoria's most famous town. The drive there is a beautiful one, over good roads; and the hairpin bends are not too numerous. The view is spectacular; the thick forests, the deep valleys, the steep cliffs, and the Thompson River winding far below.

High in these North Gippsland mountains of the Great Dividing Range, much of Victoria's early history was made. Prior to disastrous bushfires which obliterated so many wayside inns and other landmarks, the old road from Mansfield to Walhalla was one of the most romantic highways in Victoria. The district embraces the ghost towns and villages of Woods Point, Gaffney's Creek, Aberfeldy, Ten Mile, and Jamieson: relics of the hectic goldmining era, each with its own colourful history.

The charming little township of Jamieson, which lies in a peaceful valley amost encircled by towering mountains, has developed into a quiet holiday resort, favoured by anglers. Its Junction Hotel, more than a century old, has outlived all but one of its many competitors; at one time two local breweries, as well as those of Melbourne, were needed to keep up supplies for the thirsty miners. In 1860, apart from hotels, the main street of Jamieson was replete with stores, billiard saloons, dancing-halls, and all the trappings typical of goldmining towns of those days. Jamieson was an important centre from which pack-horse services radiated to the diggings in the surrounding country. Some of those tortuous mountain tracks can still be seen.

While Jamieson was being dug for its hidden wealth, other prospectors were pushing farther afield, hopeful that they would strike richer bonanzas. The hamlet of Woods Point owes its birth to the discovery of gold there by Joseph Corry and his German mate, Dittmer Behrens. The difficulties that faced them would have daunted any but the most courageous. Lured on by the golden magnet that had drawn men from all parts of the world in search of treasure in the new southern land, they struggled forward with their heavy loads over precipitous mountains, and hacked their way through dense forest. Each man hoped that, beyond the next mountain, the great nugget of which all miners dreamt might be at the bottom of a shallow creek; or that there might be a fabulously rich reef in the mountainside itself.

Nearing the source of the Goulburn River, the two men decided to separate, Corry to prospect the right branch of the stream, and Behrens the left. They were to meet at a certain landmark on the summit of the ranges. During the same day, Corry, because of the steepness of the mountain terrain, was compelled to make a detour over a mountain spur. Descending into a sharp gully his keen eyes detected a patch of loose quartz, in which he thought he saw a golden glitter. Approaching closer, he was overjoyed to find that the stone was studded with specks that he knew without doubt to be gold. The elated prospector clambered with renewed energy to a peak where he could cooee to his mate; it was not long before the two men had set to work to test the find. The yield of gold from their first efforts was richly rewarding, and so the first claim at Woods Point was pegged out.

Joseph Corry called his mine the *Morning Star*, and it brought him great riches. A company eventually took the mine over, and by 1903 it had yielded gold to the value—in those days—of two million pounds. There were other rich mines in the district. One of the lucky miners was Tom Cherry, who made £140,000 —an amount which would be of very much greater value today. Another was Tim Hurley, who made a fortune and returned to his native village in Ireland, where he staggered his friends with his immense wealth.

Nothing could stop the fortune-hunters. They struggled over the wild mountainous country with their families and their belongings, in all sorts of contraptions. A shrewd storekeeper, Henry Woods, after whom the district is named, built the first store on a point of the nearest mountain. Other storekeepers and tradesmen were quick to follow the diggers to the new goldfields. Many of the mines bore names embodying the nostalgia of their owners: Harp of Erin, Alabama, Germania, Rose of Denmark, the Canadian, China, Rose, Shamrock and Thistle.

One famous character, Bessie the Barmaid, was known as the

Queen of Woods Point, and retired with a fortune. Engaged by a publican at Woods Point, she was *en route* from Melbourne when she arrived at one of the last and steepest mountains before her destination. An enterprising Frenchman had established a monopoly of pack-horse transport over the mountains, his charges being sixpence per pound on all freight, whether human or material. Fourteen-stone Bessie argued that the charge was exorbitant, and considered turning back when the carrier refused any concession. However, she paid up, and was delivered safely over the mountain to what was to prove for the buxom Bessie a case of over the mountain to the pot of gold.

An 1862 copy of the newspaper, the *Woods Point Times and Mountaineer*, contains some quaint advertisements. One notifies the public that Richard Hoskins delivers 'fresh and genuine milk' in the town every morning. Another, inserted by the Town Crier, states: 'I beg to inform the public that I have just received from Melbourne a fine, mellow-toned bell, without flaw or blemish, and having practised my calling for some hours a day, I now respectfully solicit the patronage of those requiring my services.'

As the mines petered out and the diggers started to move off to other fields, the town dwindled year by year, with the forest ever regaining its supremacy. One by one the six banks, the State and private schools, the hospital and churches, closed their doors. Nevertheless, the reopening of the original *Morning Star* mine in recent years has forged a link with Woods Point's golden past.

The gateway to East Gippsland is Sale, the administrative capital of Gippsland. A cathedral city, Sale is the centre of rich grazing land and of a multi-million dollar irrigation scheme. Its secondary industries include the manufacture of butter, flour, bacon, engineering products, plastics ,and cement tiles. The city is linked with Lakes Entrance not only by road, but by water, over a distance of sixty-one miles, connecting with the Gippsland Lakes. It is possible to travel on the lakes by launch all the way from Sale—or Bairnsdale—to the Southern Ocean at Lakes Entrance. The simple loveliness of the Gippsland

Lakes, stretching for fifty miles, parallel to the Ninety Mile Beach, is their greatest enchantment. The wooded shoreline is very beautiful and the streams that flow into the lakes, including the Mitchell, Nicholson and Tambo Rivers, are the home of the majestic fighting fish, the Great Southern Bream.

Sale was known to the Aborigines around the area as 'Way-put.' The first settler in the district was Archibald McIntosh, who took up a property by a creek. This flooded soon after his arrival, and the area was subsequently known as 'Flooding Creek'. In the early days, the town was also known as 'The Heart', a name given by Governor La Trobe, who stated in a letter written in 1844 that, the district 'may truly be called the heart of Gippsland'. The present name was adopted in a burst of patriotic fervour soon after receipt of the news of the death of 'Fighting Bob' (Sir Robert Henry Sale), who was mortally wounded at Moodkee, India, in 1845. After the seige of Jellalabad, Lady Sale and others were placed as hostages with Akbar Khan and, although a terrible massacre occurred, she survived and was rescued eight months later.

There was a time, before forest spoliation made its mark, when some of the world's tallest trees grew in Gippsland— eucalypts exceeding four hundred feet in height. Here is what Baron von Mueller, botanist and explorer, wrote in 1870: 'On the Black Spur Range, Gippsland, is a gumtree, alive, measuring 420 foot in height, whilst lying on the ground nearby is one the almost incredible height of 480 feet.'

A Gippsland tree, five hundred feet in height, was officially recorded by William G. Robinson, of Berwick, on a journey from Gippsland to Mount Baw Baw. He personally measured the giant. Alas, bushfires and the work of man in clearing the forests have done their work all too well.

East Gippsland was the setting for what seems to be the most authentic story concerning the term, 'Waltzing Matilda'. Certainly it was handed down as a folk tale among the settlers in this district of tall timber. Matilda is said to have been the first woman swaggie to be seen in Victoria. She and her husband, Joe, were very well known and respected throughout East Gippsland; their surname was unknown, and the wife was always called Mrs Swaggie Joe.

Matilda and Joe were entirely happy in their carefree life, wandering the old bush tracks winter and summer; Joe with his bluey on his back, Matilda with a smaller swag on hers. Matilda often told how her father reacted when Joe asked him for his daughter's hand: 'What! My daughter marry a common swaggie! A man who can't offer her even a shack to live in! Do you think I'd let you go a-waltzing Matilda all over the countryside?'

Despite this opposition, the girl married Joe and set off with him on a lifetime of wandering through the spacious countryside, which they understood and loved with all their hearts.

Eventually the day came when they grew infirm, their youthful strength and vigour sapped by the years. They were offered a home by a kindly couple living at Bruthen, but they refused it, saying that they could never live indoors like other folks, and they would go on until they came to the end of the track.

Then, one sad day, Matilda was taken ill in the morning and died at midday. Swaggie Joe dug her grave at the foot of an old gum tree and sat with his arms about her until it grew dark. Then he buried her.

Next morning, as he prepared to fasten on his bluey, he muttered, 'Oh well, Bluey, you'll have to be Matilda to me now, and we'll waltz along together 'til the end.'

Swaggie Joe's name for his bluey was soon adopted by other sundowners. 'Waltzing the bluey' was already their idiom for tramping with their swag, so it was not long before it evolved into 'Waltzing Matilda'. It is said that Joe developed the habit of talking to his swag when alone in the bush. He was sometimes seen with it propped against a tree while he talked to it, addressing it as 'Matilda'.

Perched on a spur of the Great Dividing Range in the central highlands region, seventy-five miles by rail north-west of Melbourne, is the town of Daylesford. In earlier years it was an important mining centre, and in the 1880s it had a population of many thousands. Today there are woollen mills in the town, and much of the surrounding land is given to agriculture. The district, too, is a popular holiday resort, the mountain scenery, lakes and mineral springs at Hepburn—two miles distant—attracting many visitors.

The town was first known as the Jim Crow diggings, the name being derived from a music-hall song of the day. Precious stones, including sapphires and rubies, have been found in the district and some gold is still produced. Indeed, people in Daylesford and its sister town Hepburn will tell you that the surrounding hills contain more gold than was ever dug out of them. The reason for this claim is that mines in the area were worked for more than seventy years, and were discontinued in the belief that the sinking of shafts was interfering with the flow of mineral water, which was considered, at that time, more valuable to the community than gold.

It was a big event in Daylesford when its Theatre Royal was opened on 5 December, 1864. The notorious Lola Montez performed there for the delight of the miners; her 'spider dance' was always a riot with the diggers. Almost every nationality was represented in the camp at Jim Crow diggings, where the gold rush reached its peak in 1853. There were said to be some 20,000 Europeans and 5,000 Chinese.

Hepburn was originally called Spring Creek, because of its many springs, some of them flowing from the rocks. Their source is still undetermined; but the main belief is that they are fed from a natural reservoir in the volcanic opening that once existed in Mount Franklin, a long-extinct volcano. The Aborigines knew the area as Moorekyle, and the present name honours Captain John Hepburn. The Captain was a Scots member of the party who took the first cattle overland from Sydney to Port Phillip—taking three months to make the trip—and who eventually established the first settlement at Hepburn in 1838.

There was a time when Hepburn played its part in establishing Australia's cricket-bat industry—an industry which once supplied the world. The Crockett willow plantation near the town contains over 5,000 willow trees, which were grown from one small cutting sent from England. For many years the plantation supplied Australia and other cricket-conscious lands with willow for cricket bats.

Spa water and the mineral springs of Hepburn brought booming business for thirty years or more, and still draw the health-seeker. The true Hepburnites have been visiting the district for years and years. They sip the waters of the eternal, crystal-clear springs and assess their quality and 'bouquet' with the discriminating palate of a wine-taster. Their daily ritual is a visit to the springs before breakfast, often carrying bottles of the water back to their temporary abode. Such dedicated Hepburnites will tell you of the power of good the water has done for their rheumatism, arthritis, random aches and pains and general debility; and of its producing an overall sense of well-being.

A large overseas investment company once tried to buy out the whole area so that they could commercialize the springs, which are equal to the best anywhere. Because of so much local opposition, the proposed scheme fell through. Perhaps the day will come when the Hepburn-Daylesford districts, with their 80 per cent of Australia's known mineral springs, will become a world-class spa resort.

Right now, Hepburn appeals strongly to the trout angler and those who like to get away from it all. There is a sense of isolation and calm detachment, the crisp and aromatic air adding pleasure to the locality's high altitude, rolling hills, deep gullies and winding walks. And always there is the refreshing aroma which arises, possibly, from the rich, brown, mineral-impregnated soil of the volcanic surroundings.

TWENTY-THREE

Cobb and Co.

WESTWARDS through central Victoria, the highlands of the Great Dividing Range fall away to a little more than 1,200 feet in the Kilmore Gap, 42 miles north of Melbourne, and then end spectacularly in the Grampians. Through this gap in the Great Divide pass the main road and railway between Melbourne and Sydney.

The town of Kilmore is the centre of a rich pastoral, agricultural, and dairying area. Because of the great fertility of its volcanic soil the district was occupied by squatters from New South Wales from as early as 1837. In 1841 a land speculator named William Routledge purchased a property of eight square miles and named it Kilmore, after his birthplace in County Cavan, Ireland. He subdivided this estate and leased or sold farm-blocks, mainly to Irish immigrants, who cleared the land of the rocks and used them for fencing their properties; these are still a feature of the district.

One of the 1840 migrants was a young man who took sheep to the Kilmore district and established himself as a squatter. After a couple of years he abandoned pastoral life and went to Tasmania, where he entered politics, eventually becoming Premier. This was Sir Adye Douglas who for more than fifty years played a notable part in the public affairs of Tasmania.

The little settlement at Kilmore made good progress, and during the 1850s flourished as a market town and depot for the gold-diggings. With the building of St. Patrick's church in

1857, Kilmore became the first Catholic parish to be established in Victoria, outside the metropolitan area. A Cobb and Co. coach service began to operate daily from Melbourne to Kilmore in 1854. The Coach routes were later extended to the north; but Kilmore retained its importance, since it was the first staging-point north of Melbourne.

From the 1850s onward, the story of coaching in Australia is essentially the story of Cobb and Co. The first of the important gold finds in Victoria was made in 1851. As the news of the discoveries spread, tens of thousands of newcomers from all parts of the world poured into the country, nearly all rushing to the goldfields at Ballarat, Bendigo, Mount Alexander, Beechworth, and other diggings.

Many gold diggers in California, who were having little success there, decided to come to Victoria and try their luck on the new fields. Freeman Cobb, a young American coach driver for the Adams and Co. Express in the United States, became very enthusiastic about the possibility of repeating in Victoria what the company had done in California. He persistently approached the heads of the firm to undertake the venture, and send him to Australia to launch it. Eventually the company gave way, and agreed to send him out to investigate the position.

A coach, and four other American drivers, arrived in Port Melbourne by a later ship; but in the meantime, the Adams Co. Express had abandoned the idea of running a coach service. This, of course, left Cobb and the others out of a job. They decided to pool their resources, run the service themselves, and pay the company for the cost of the coach and horses out of their earnings.

Cobb drove during the first journey from Fishermen's Bend to Melbourne, a distance of five miles; and the coach was packed with inside and outside passengers. The fare was £2 per passenger (and his luggage.) Most of the miners walked to the fields. If they were lucky, they arranged to have their swags and belongings carried by bullock-dray, which at first was the chief means of transport.

As the coach journeyed on to Melbourne, a 25-year-old American stood aside to let it pass. He had come from America on the same ship as Freeman Cobb eight months earlier. He had a spade, pick and wash pan, and the neat swag of an experienced fossicker. His name was James Rutherford, and he looked at the coach with far-seeing eyes. He said afterwards that he had the strange impression that he saw a rainbow above the coach. If he did it was a rainbow which led him to riches, for later he became the head of Cobb and Co., which in its heyday was the largest single transport business in the world.

For each of the American drivers, the decision to carry on the project themselves was fortunate: for Australia, it was historic, and brought organized transport to this country. Within seven days, the first Cobb and Co. coach ran to Geelong. The fare over the badly cut-up track was £15, and was willingly paid by passengers seeking their fortunes on the diggings. As the little company progressed, Cobb purchased the best horses and imported more American coaches after the smartest model, and still smarter Yankee drivers with them. Good horses, strong coaches, and experienced drivers were needed for the terrible roads of those days.

At the beginning of Cobb and Co's history the drivers were all Americans; most of them had been engaged in a similar capacity with Wells Fargo and Co., the largest coaching business in America. Those drivers were young, strong men whose handling of large teams of six and seven horses was a science new to Australia. They were paid wages which were quite fabulous for those times—up to £20 a week—and were all given free meals and accommodation by the proprietors of the coaching inns.

When the coach came to any very steep hills, the driver would pull up and insert steel shoes or turned-up plates under the wheels; they were attached to the coach by means of stout chains. The coach would then skid down: a very simple and effective technique, especially when the coach had a full load. It inspired confidence in the passengers to know that the driver was not relying entirely on his brakes. Reaching the bottom, the coach would again be stopped, the shoes withdrawn, and the journey resumed.

The Australian employees—the grooms—were not accustomed initially to handling six, eight and twelve horses from a box seat; but they soon learned the handling of the reins. Apt pupils, they quickly became as efficient as their American instructors, and then there were no finer drivers on the roads than these Australian-born. Some of the worst roads in Victoria were found in Gippsland, and became a by-word to all drivers. Especially notorious were the Brandy Creek and Shady Creek roads. An inn—a mere bark hut—was erected on each road with a bullock waggon in readiness night and day to haul vehicles out of the permanent surrounding bogs.

In 1861, the other American, James Rutherford, comes again into the story. On his arrival in Melbourne—he was born in New York—he had immediately gone into the bush to study life in Australia. He broke in horses, worked as a stockman, and did bush work of all kinds. As a result he knew the country, the roads, and where the best horses were to be had.

The business of Cobb and Co. had changed twice (one buyer holding it only for a month), when it was taken over by a company consisting of James Rutherford and five others. Among them was Walter Russell Hall, who later made a fortune out of gold, and gave his name to the $2 million Walter and Eliza Hall Trust in Melbourne. Freeman Cobb, when he returned to the United States, had a nice little fortune, and afterwards became a Senator for Massachusetts.

Rutherford kept to Cobb's slogan, 'Follow the Gold'; but he reorganized and extended the Victorian services, and secured a monopoly of the mail contracts. Under his expert management the company became so big that by 1870 it was harnessing 6,000 horses daily, had 4,000 others in reserve in stables and in paddocks, and covered 28,000 miles a week, collecting £95,000 a year in mail subsidies. It had a payroll exceeding £100,000 per annum.

Thus Cobb and Co. was responsible for opening up new farms along the route; staging-hostels were established every ten to twenty miles; indirect employment was created in road-building, horse farms, fodder stores, stables, saddlery shops and coach-building firms. With Rutherford at the helm, the organization quickly moved to a dominant position in Australian land transport. Its genius for service, and its adaptability in the face of increasing railway competition, allowed it to maintain its position for nearly seventy years; and it was not until 1924—when ousted by the service-car rather than the railway—that the last Cobb and Co. coach ran.

It was in Ballarat that Rutherford caused a coach to be built which was the largest ever seen in Australia, and quite possibly, in the whole world. It was named the 'Leviathan' and was built to seat 72 passengers in comfort, although on occasions 100 persons were packed inside and outside the huge vehicle. Twenty-two horses running in pairs were harnessed to it, and, to manage the long team, four postillions were required, in addition to the driver. The coach itself was twenty-five feet long and had plate glass windows. The famous coach painter, Ned Chester, was commissioned to paint and decorate it.

The coach provided a striking display at the first Melbourne Cup. An unofficial Melbourne Cup had been run the year before, but the first Tuesday in November 1861 saw fleets of special coaches running a crowd of 4,000 people to Flemington. They were going to see, not only the races, but also a display of the handling of big coach teams, which Cobb and Co. had promised.

Although the American drivers were masters at handling the reins, it was announced that Edward Devine, better known as 'Cabbage-tree Ned', who was to become the most famous of all Australian coaching drivers, would take 'Leviathan', the monster coach, to the course. Cheers arose from the Flat and Leger when the great vehicle and its twenty-two horses came swinging on to the course and sped along the track. Crowds in the stands, which exceeded all estimates, were excited long before the first race.

Then followed eight-in-hands driven by the Americans. Levi Rich, a leather-faced man with a wide sombrero, drove the first of these, swinging his team of beautifully-groomed blacks through the gateway and on to the course in front of the stands. Ike Haig followed with another; and then came two more, with Big Sampson and Eddie Winkler at the reins.

All four coaches carried passengers. Suddenly, to the surprise and delight of the onlookers, these brilliant drivers began describing figures of eight, keeping time to the strains of the band playing in the main enclosure. Then these four eight-in-hands paired off and gave a startling and picturesque exhibition of mammoth dancing to partners. Each pair, racing side by side, dashed across the tracks of the other pair, swung out into graceful curves away from each other, and converged again at the top of the figure eight.

The crowd went wild with delight as the respective pairs kept level, and the drivers with unerring accuracy, steered teams which twisted and interwove in this amazing dance of the horses. And these were the men and animals whose daily job was the rather prosaic one of carrying men and His Majesty's mails. But Cobb and Co. coaches were never prosaic to those who loved horses, and travelling over long distances in a new and unspoiled land, whether by day or under the stars, and even if the roads were rough.

Ned Devine included amongst his passengers the first English cricket team to visit Australia. He drove them throughout their tour; and at its conclusion was the guest of honour at a banquet in Geelong, where he was given a purse of 300 sovereigns. He died at Ballarat on 18 December, 1909, and was buried in Ballarat cemetery; the grave now carries a memorial erected by public subscription.

The original Cobb and Co. operated only in Victoria, the goldfields traffic being the backbone of Victorian coaching activities. As the railways extended to the mining centres, coaches lost their importance. In 1861, Rutherford transferred the company to New South Wales; and during the 1880s the greatest development of the business was in Queensland, where before the end of that decade 4,000 miles of coach-route were controlled by Cobb and Co.

As new railways were constructed, the coach-routes were pushed farther out to serve the back country; and they were partly instrumental in opening up these areas for settlement, by establishing reliable communication between them and the centres of supply. Many half-way houses depended on the coaching traffic for a livelihood, and disappeared as the coaches were withdrawn.

The old coaching days of Cobb and Co. have held a special appeal for Australian poets, notably Henry Lawson and Will Ogilvie. The latter wrote in his, *The Lights of Cobb and Co,*:

By north and south, by east and west
  By dawn and dark of day,
By swamps and plains, and mountain crest
  They take the foremost way,
And where the slanting sunrays dip,
  And underneath the stars,
Is heard the cracking of the whip,
  And creaking of the bars.

And out beyond the reach of rail
  As far as wheel tracks go,
The drovers round their campfire hail
  The lights of Cobb and Co.
The settlers wait at close of day,
  To hear the rolling wheels,
When faintly through the twilight grey,
  The far whip challenge steals.

They take the messages of love,
  And bring them safely through,
The faithful sun that shines above,
  Is not more loyal true,
They bear the lines of hope and trust,
  The words of weal and woe,
And life itself was trusted in
  The hands of Cobb and Co.

TWENTY-FOUR

Mountains of the Dreamtime

On 11 July, 1836, near the termination of the Great Dividing Range in western Victoria, Sir Thomas Mitchell, the notable overlander, obtained his first view of the mountains he was to name 'Grampians'. That day, he wrote in his diary: 'From a high forest hill I first obtained a complete view of a noble range of mountains . . . presenting as bold and picturesque an outline as ever painter imagined.'

The Aboriginal tribesmen knew this strange, beautiful region which they called 'The Mountains of the Dreamtime'. Here they sheltered in the many caves, some of which still show examples of their stone-age art painted on the walls: ochre prints of the artists' hands, and symbols of the Dreamtime—the time before man's creation.

The Grampians embrace an area of about 400 square miles of the Great Divide, and their hard sandstone composition has been weathered throughout the ages into fantastic shapes, and slashed by chasms and gorges, deep and vertical, trapping the moisture for the thick and lush vegetation. They consist of three main ranges, bold and varied in outline. Laid down aeons ago, layer upon layer, on the bottom of an ancient sea, the ranges stretch north and south for about sixty miles. In the course of time, a great upheaval occurred, tilting the beds towards the west at an angle of about thirty degrees. Most of the ranges have sharp peaks with long slopes on one side and steep cliffs on the

170

other where the sandstone beds break off abruptly. The bold escarpments afford an excellent example of differential erosion on tilted rock layers; as does the fractured, low domed plateau forming the Dundas Highlands.

Some granite is interspersed among the Grampians, but sandstone predominates. It has provided splendid building stone; the Victorian Houses of Parliament are constructed of Grampians freestone that has weathered to a soft grey colour.

The flora of the Grampians is renowned. There are nearly 800 species, some of which are found nowhere else in the world —a treasure-trove for the botanist, and a delight to the visitor. Some seventy species of orchids in the rock crannies and valleys of the mountains provide a succession of blooms throughout the year, while in spring and early summer the Grampians are decked with a floral mantle of heaths of every tint, from snowy white to richest crimson. The beauty of the wildflowers is revealed in golden wattle, boronias, fuchsias, grevillias, and thryptomene, adorning the long sloping valleys, the precipitous walls and the craggy summits of this undisturbed land of the Dreamtime.

Undisturbed, it is; except for a tourist centre at Hall's Gap in the Fyans Valley, the junction of three main ranges. From this, well-defined paths lead to waterfalls, canyons, panoramic lookouts, and the unique formations carved by time and the elements from the great rock walls. Only a generation ago, the Grampians were relatively inaccessible, but today they are traversed by modern motor roads. These connect with the adjacent towns of Ararat, Stawell, Horsham, Hamilton, Dunkeld, Natimuk, and Balmoral.

Ararat is a modern town of 8,000 people in the centre of a rich wheat and woolgrowing district. Several large vineyards lie not far from the town, the most important being the Great Western, whose underground cellars are among the largest in Australia. Ararat had its beginnings in the gold discovery of 1854. It soon petered out; but a new strike in the following year started one of the greatest gold rushes Australia has ever seen. The discovery was made by Chinese, and within a matter of weeks a large portion of the total population of Victoria was under canvas at Ararat. From the Canton Lead—the Chinese mine—3,000 ounces of gold were taken in three weeks. Ararat (the original name of Armenia), and Mount Ararat, were named by an early squatter who rested there after a weary overland journey. The Aborigines knew the district as Butingitch.

Hamilton, proclaimed a city in 1949, has had a long and historic association with the development of the Western District. The area was discovered by Sir Thomas Mitchell, who crossed the site of Hamilton in 1836 and, as with the Grampians, bestowed a Scottish name, christening a little stream, 'Grange Burn'. For many years, Hamilton was known as 'The Grange'. The first settlers were the Hentys, in 1837. Apart from the Grampians, natural features of the picturesque countryside include the Wannon and Nigretta Falls, Lake Surprise atop of Mount Eccles, and Mount Napier, one of the last active volcanoes in Victoria.

Hamilton and other areas adjacent to the Grampians were all serviced by Cobb and Co's coaches. From Ballarat westwards, the coaches ran to Hamilton via Dunkeld, and Hamilton became a centre serving Balmoral and Harrow, among other towns. Even when the railway reached Hamilton in 1877, Cobb and Co. served as a feeder. The company, at the height of its Hamilton service, had two offices in the town, one at French Street and the other near the post office. The Hamilton Historical Society erected in 1958 a commemorative plaque to Cobb and Co., on the site of the stables built in 1856, which had housed the horses of the Melbourne Royal Mail. There is in existence in Hamilton a Cobb and Co. ticket issued in 1882 for the journey from Ararat to Stawell; it cost £1, and the distance was between 18 to 20 miles.

A new Cobb and Co. coach was sent from Hamilton to meet two young Royal Dukes—Prince Albert and Prince George—who made a tour of a considerable part of Australia in 1881. They did the sea voyage in the H.M.S. *Bacchante*, leaving the vessel at Fremantle, and journeying to Penola. There they were met by the coach with its spanking team of four very smart greys. When the young Princes arrived at Hamilton they were happily seated on the box seat with the driver, whom they said was, 'a corker of a driver'.

Deserted mine near Tenterfield, New South Wales, a relic of the long-forgotten mining boom (page 62)

Dreaming of its past and still hoping for a future in gold. Walhalla, Victoria, produced 100 tons of gold   (page 155)

The 'Leviathan' coach of Cobb and Co. on occasions carried 100 persons   (page 167)

Finding of Australia's 'Babes in the Wood', as depicted by S. T. Gill, the goldfields artist   (page 175)

Although web-footed, the Cape Barren Goose is rarely seen on the water, but feeds on grasses and herbage   (page 177)

Kangaroos are timid creatures, yet when hunted and brought to bay they will attack, kicking forward with telling effect   (page 16)

Cobb and Co. not only serviced the north, north-west and west of Victoria; they were established in the east as well, right through Gippsland, and even in the mountains. Wherever there was a road with a town at the end of it, there you would find Cobb and Co. rendering excellent service. If gold was being obtained, so much the better; for the prospector and digger were always good paying passengers.

The town of Stawell is the main eastern approach to the Grampians; and its proximity to the ranges makes it a natural starting place for mountain tours. The Western Highway passes through the town, whose district is engaged in wool-growing and in the production of apples, fat lambs, poultry, and wheat; although to a lesser extent. Secondary industries include woollen-manufacture, flour-milling, brick-making, timber-milling, butter-making, and the manufacture of pre-fabricated houses.

Stawell is famous in sporting circles for the Stawell Gift foot-race. Run over a distance of 130 yards, and held annually on Easter Monday, it attracts professional runners from all parts of Australia. Held in the town's delightful Central Park, it is the blue-ribbon event of the professional foot-running world.

The history of the settlement goes back to 1851, when gold was discovered in the vicinity. Settlers first knew Stawell as Pleasant Creek, and the Aborigines called the site Kobram. Its present name honours Sir William Foster Stawell, who was the first Attorney-General of Victoria as a separate colony. He drafted the Victorian Constitution Act, and became the first Chief Justice. Twenty thousand miners streamed into the Stawell diggings during the first big rush in the 1850s; and some of the deepest shafts in the world were sunk there.

Balmoral, named after the royal residence in Scotland, and known to the Aboriginal tribes in the area as 'Daarangurt', is a small pastoral and agricultural district on the Glenelg River. Rocklands reservoir, nine miles from Balmoral, forms part of the largest irrigation system in the Southern Hemisphere. The reservoir is located at the southern edge of the formidable Black Range; it draws its water from the Glenelg River, rising in the Victoria Valley of the Grampians. A mighty wall of concrete, 103 feet high and 70 feet thick, holds back the 25 square miles of impounded water. Sportsmen regard the area, with its camping and boating facilities, as their idea of heaven.

A feature of Dunkeld (named after Dunkeld in Perthshire), is the bird and animal life. Immediately at the back of Dunkeld, which is on the Glenelg Highway, rise the peaks of Mount Sturgeon and Mount Abrupt. From the latter, the striking serrated peaks of the Serra Range come into view. A government tourist brochure on the towns of the Grampians mentions that Dunkeld's Mount Sturgeon was so called from its likeness to the fish of that name. This is not so; the mountain was named by Mitchell in 1835, after Colonel Sturgeon, a brother officer.

Approximately twenty miles from the most northerly ramparts of the Grampians is the city of Horsham, the metropolis of the rich and progressive Wimmera region. The city has a population of more than 9,000. The public buildings are handsome, and the city is well-endowed with parks and botanic gardens. Three golf courses, an Olympic-size swimming pool, bowls, croquet, tennis, and a light aero club cater for the recreation of the citizens and visitors.

Wheat-growing and sheep-raising are the principal industries of the district, water for the farms being obtained from the Wimmera-Mallee system. Supplies from this same source are also used for irrigating some 3,000 acres of land, where fruit, vegetables and tomatoes are cultivated. Secondary industries of Horsham include flour-milling, founding, and the manufacture of butter, hosiery, and plaster.

The first settler in the district was James Monckton Darlot, who in 1841 selected a property near the present city, and named it after his native Horsham in Sussex, England. (The old English meaning of Horsham was 'horse enclosure'.) The Aboriginal name for the area was *Bongamilor*, meaning 'place of flowers'. The first newspaper, the *Horsham Times*, was established in 1873—six years before the railway from Melbourne was opened—and is still in existence. Near Horsham is the Longerenong Agricultural College, which specializes in the agriculture of North-Western Victoria.

Sir Samuel Wilson, in partnership with his brothers, bought a station property here, and in 1868–69 became the sole owner. *Longerenong*, an Aboriginal word, has some significance, therefore, since it means 'part or divide'. Sir Samuel made a gift of £30,000 to the Melbourne University, where Wilson Hall is named in his honour. He first came to Australia in 1852 and interested himself in the breeding of sheep, angora goats, salmon, trout, and—of all things—ostriches. Wilson amassed a vast fortune; he paid £236,000 for Ercildoune, near Ballarat, which was then the highest price ever given in Australia for a station property.

He was an active member of the Acclimatization Society of Victoria, and in 1873 wrote pamphlets on the angora goat and the ostrich. Five years later, he produced a book on the introduction of the Californian salmon into Victoria; another edition entitled, *Salmon at the Antipodes*, was published in London in 1879. His knighthood was bestowed on him in the same year that he was elected a member of the Legislative Council of Victoria.

On the perimeter of the Grampians, fifteen miles west of Horsham, lies the township of Natimuk, with its great 900 acres stretch of water, Natimuk Lake. Mount Arapiles, rising to a height of 700 feet above the plains, is a striking feature in sandstone. From the summit, there are fine views of the surrounding country including dozens of miniature salt lakes and the serrated peaks of the Grampians cutting the horizon.

The Wimmera district to the west of Natimuk was the setting for the drama of Australia's 'Babes in the Wood'. These children were Isaac Duff, aged nine, his four-year old brother Frank, and the seven-year old sister, Jane. One mid-winter's day in 1864, the three little children set out to gather wild heath to make brooms. They had a happy time picking the heath and chasing butterflies, and they enjoyed their simple lunch of bread and treacle.

But by the time the evening shadows were falling, they found that they had taken the wrong direction for home; and realized that they were lost. They cooeed for their father, but the only answer came from howling dingoes. Exhausted and frightened, the children huddled at the foot of a tree and said the prayers their mother had taught them, before her death.

Then began the heart-breaking story of the children's sufferings. Day after day they staggered through the forest, their only food being wild berries, leaves, and wattle gum. Their only drink was dew, which they licked off the plants. The weather was bitterly cold; and each night when they lay down exhausted, Jane took off her dress and wrapped it around her baby brother. Then she covered him and the other boy with leaves to keep them warm.

Meanwhile their grief-stricken father had organized a search party of twenty men; but after seven days the searchers abandoned their efforts because of heavy rain. The father persisted, however, and secured the aid of three Aborigines to track the children.

Eight days after their disappearance, one of the natives picked up the mark of a little boot, remarking: 'Here two big ones carry little one.' They followed the staggering foot-prints of the children, and inspected the beds of bush and leaves that Jane had made for the baby boy. 'Here they plenty tired. Not much longer now.' At nightfall, one of the Aborigines tracking the footprints suddenly pointed. There lay the three pale, skeleton-like children on the ground.

'Dead! My poor babies—they're dead!' sobbed their broken-hearted father. But, miraculously, it was found that there was life in all three of them. They were unconscious, and hovered between life and death for weeks, despite every care and medical attention. However, eventually they recovered.

When the story of these brave little Australians was published, the people of Victoria regarded Jane as a national heroine; and in 1865, a painting of the episode by the goldfields' artist, S. T. Gill, won considerable popularity. Queen Victoria wrote them a personal letter, and Sir Phillip Dalziel ordered a marble statue to be sculpted of the three children sleeping among the leaves. When completed, it was presented to Jane.

Jane lived to the age of seventy-five. She died a poor and forgotten woman, and was buried at Horsham. Only leaves and grasses, such as she once spread over her brothers, covered her grave. However, in recent years, admirers of this heroine subscribed and purchased a headstone commemorating her bravery, which was placed over her grave.

Of the 395 species of birds native to Victoria, at least 100 are to be found in the Grampians. Many introduced birds have also made the Grampians their home. The sweet flute notes of the Harmonious Thrush accord him pride of place among the bird songsters, which include the Larks, Jays, and Bell Birds. Other beautiful birds of the Grampians are the Blue Kingfishers, Bronzewing Pigeons, Honeyeaters, Fairy Wrens, Yellow-breasted Robins, and the Cape Barren Geese. The latter, a handsome and intensely interesting species, is an anomalous bird, related to the extinct giant goose of New Zealand; but with no living allies.

On the open heath flats, emus may be seen in large numbers. In the Victoria and Wartook Valleys, the Great-grey or Forester kangaroo may frequently be observed in mobs of up to fifty. These valleys are the home also of red deer; while the always-appealing koala can be seen in the vicinity of Hall's Gap and Lake Wartook.

Present in the streams of the Grampians are the duck-billed platypus and the interesting, but little-known, water-rat. Australian water-rats evolved from an ancient rodent invasion and became adapted to aquatic life over the centuries. Their heads are streamlined; the broad and paddle-like feet are partly webbed; and their fur is seal-like. At night the water-rats inhabit swamps, streams, and estuaries, feeding on insects, mussels and other aquatic animals, and making their burrows on swamp and river edges.

The platypus and the water-rat are the subjects of a fascinating Aboriginal legend, which—like all their myths and folk tales—explained to the people's own mental satisfaction the wonderful and extraordinary natural system of which they were an inseparable part:

In the long long ago, there was a young and foolish duck named Tharalkoo who used to swim by herself in a certain billabong. Now this was a dangerous habit for any duck at any time, because this particular stretch of water was reputed to be the home of Mulloka, the water-devil, and it was especially unwise as Tharalkoo was a really attractive young duck. Her tribe warned her repeatedly against her foolish practice, but she disregarded the advice and, with a toss of her head and a scornful quack, would be off to swim in the dark waters of the shunned billabong.

There came a day when this headstrong young duck swam far down the billabong and out of sight of the camp of her people. Seeing a patch of tender young grass on the bank she moved over to it to rest and feed. Little did she know that beneath this bank was the burrow where Biggoon the giant water-rat had made his home. He had been watching Tharalkoo, and while she was feeding on the lush grass he rushed out of his burrow and seized her.

All of Tharalkoo's struggles and crying were in vain. Biggoon shouted in a terrible voice: 'You are mine, all mine! I want a wife! I'm tired of living alone!' Tharalkoo begged him to let her go. She pleaded that she must return to her tribe because a marriage mate had already been chosen for her. But Biggoon refused to listen and roared: 'You must stay here and be my wife! I'm lonely and tired of living here without a wife to prepare my food and care for me!'

Moreover, Biggoon warned Tharalkoo that if she made any attempt to escape he would kill her with the spear that he always carried with him. Tharalkoo, although thoroughly terrified, tried to scare him by saying that her tribe would surely come looking for her and would fight and kill him. At this, Biggoon only laughed scornfully. 'Why', said he, 'they are too frightened to even look at these waters. They will think that the great Mulloka has caught you—and they know they cannot fight against him!'

And he was right. No one came searching the waters for the little lost duck. To be sure, she heard the footsteps and calls of her tribe as they looked for her in the surrounding country; but Biggoon kept her imprisoned during the day and let her out to swim only at night when he knew no one would venture from the camp for fear of Mulloka.

So it was that Tharalkoo stayed with Biggoon the water-rat and made no attempt to escape, because she knew that he was always watching her, and would never let her out of his sight for an instant. Nevertheless, Tharalkoo was a shrewd little duck and she planned to trick the water-rat. She pretended that she liked Biggoon and was happy in her new home, and she acted her part so well that the water-rat really thought she was content. To make sure, however, he pretended to take a nap in the heat of the afternoon to see if Tharalkoo tried to escape. But the little duck saw through his dodge, and was not to be tricked by it.

Convinced that Tharalkoo was happy, Biggoon began really to take an afternoon nap. This was the opportunity the duck was waiting for; and one day she crept out of the burrow and swam as fast as she could back to the camp of her people. What a great chorus of quacking greeted her return! Her former disobedience was forgotten in the general rejoicing that followed. Every one had given her up for dead, being quite certain that Mulloka, the evil spirit, had captured her.

Tharalkoo had learnt her lesson by now. She kept with the other ducks by day, for fear that the water-rat would catch her again, and never venturing out at night.

Weeks passed, and then came the breeding season. The ducks chose their nesting places, and began to busy themselves with nest building. Tharalkoo found a sheltered clump of rushes which pleased her, and so built her nest there.

Later, one by one, the proud mothers led out their broods of fluffy little ducklings. They soon marched them to the nearby creeks, edged with thick reeds, where they taught them to swim. By now every one of the mothers had shown their new ducklings, with the exception of Tharalkoo. She still remained in her hidden nest. At last her worried sisters waddled up to the reeds clump and called out to her to come out and show them her little ones.

Slowly Tharalkoo emerged from the reeds, followed by her two offspring. But what were these two tiny creatures? There was a moment's stunned silence, and then a great quacking and gabbling broke out as the ducks pushed their way and craned their necks to see the most astonishing-looking ducklings they had ever beheld.

Poor Tharalkoo pretended that she was not puzzled at the curious appearance of her young and simply said: 'These are my children.' By this time other ducks had arrived on the scene, attracted by the commotion. Never before had anyone seen the like of these strange little creatures. They were not covered with down-feathers, but had an animal coat of dense fur. Instead of having two legs, like any other decent duck, each had four. To be sure, they had duck's bills and webbed feet for swimming; but on the ankle-joints of the hind legs was a sharp point protruding through the skin. (The poor mother remembered that this was just like the points of Biggoon's spear!)

Then all the ducks set up a great clamour, demanding that these little ones should be destroyed at once. 'An evil spirit has sent them,' they cried. 'No ducklings ever looked like that! They are not of our tribe! Away with them!'

With a cry of anguish the distraught Tharalkoo snatched up her two little ones and fled . . . she knew not whither. She ran on and on until she found herself on the banks of a river, far from where her tribe dwelt, and far away from the home of Biggoon, the water-rat.

Here she remained, caring for her little ones and watching them grow bigger and stronger. Nevertheless, her heart was full of sorrow, for she missed the others of her kind; and it was not long before she died. Her children continued to thrive in the river and on its banks, and when they grew up, laid eggs and hatched out babies just like themselves. In time they became a numerous people, and were known as the tribe of Gayardaree, the platypus.

Perhaps the legend of the water-rat and the platypus was sometimes told in one of the many caves here in the Grampians —The Mountains of the Dreamtime—where our journey along the Great Divide comes to an end.

Australia differs in many ways from the other continents. While she may lack the old-world culture of other lands, she seems endowed—as though to make up for this defect—with many interesting phenomena. Our odyssey has revealed some of these things; and also some of the continent's beauty, its vast potential, its modern progress, and its people. We glimpsed a little of the geological structure of the Great Dividing Range, the unique wildlife, the bountiful earth; and we found formal and folk history commemorated wherever we travelled. Here were the backgrounds against which our actors played their almost incredible roles.

Whoever said Australia was featureless and monotonous, or her history dull?

Bibliography

Cousins, A., *The Northern Rivers of New South Wales* (1933)
McKeown, *Land of Byamee* (1938)
Phillips, H., *Historic Blue Mountains* (1938)
Trangmar, E. R., *The Saga of Cobb and Co.* (1924)
The Australian Encyclopaedia

Index

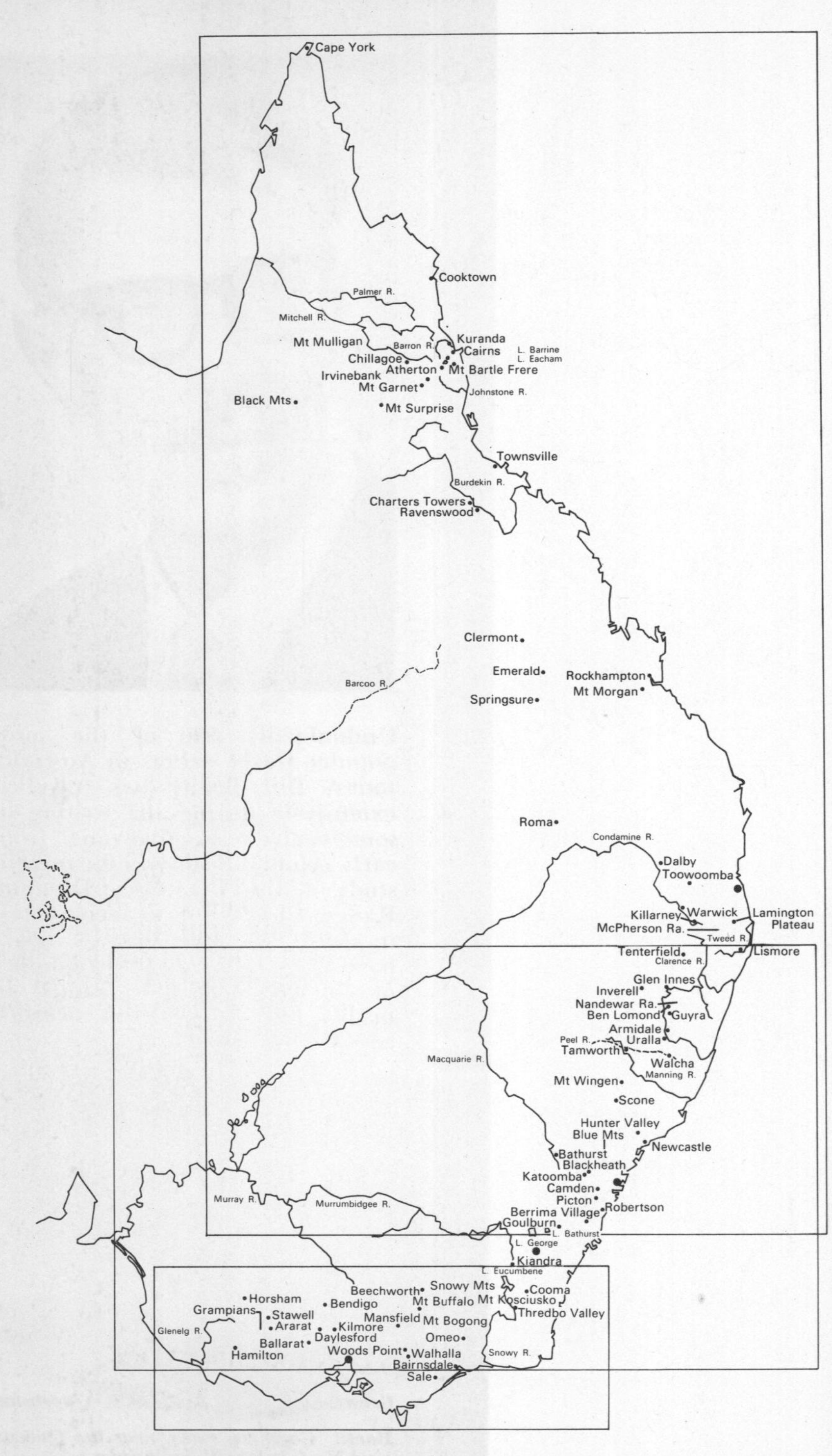

Cape York
Cooktown
Palmer R.
Mitchell R.
Mt Mulligan
Barron R.
Kuranda
Cairns
L. Barrine
L. Eacham
Chillagoe
Atherton
Mt Bartle Frere
Irvinebank
Mt Garnet
Johnstone R.
Black Mts
Mt Surprise
Townsville
Burdekin R.
Charters Towers
Ravenswood
Clermont
Emerald
Rockhampton
Barcoo R.
Springsure
Mt Morgan
Roma
Condamine R.
Dalby
Toowoomba
Killarney
Warwick
Lamington
Plateau
McPherson Ra.
Tweed R.
Tenterfield
Lismore
Clarence R.
Glen Innes
Inverell
Nandewar Ra.
Ben Lomond
Guyra
Armidale
Peel R.
Uralla
Tamworth
Walcha
Macquarie R.
Manning R.
Mt Wingen
Scone
Hunter Valley
Blue Mts
Bathurst
Newcastle
Blackheath
Katoomba
Camden
Picton
Robertson
Berrima Village
Goulburn
Murray R.
Murrumbidgee R.
L. Bathurst
L. George
Kiandra
L. Eucumbene
Beechworth
Snowy Mts
Cooma
Horsham
Bendigo
Mt Buffalo
Mt Kosciusko
Grampians
Stawell
Mansfield
Mt Bogong
Thredbo Valley
Glenelg R.
Ararat
Kilmore
Ballarat
Daylesford
Omeo
Hamilton
Woods Point
Walhalla
Snowy R.
Bairnsdale
Sale